FAMILY PRESERVATION
AND
INDIAN CHILD WELFARE

Edited by
Marc Mannes

American Indian Law Center, Inc.
Philip S. Deloria, Director

American Indian Law Center, Inc.
P.O. Box 4456 - Station A
Albuquerque, New Mexico 87196

The following people and organizations made
this guide possible:

Edited by
    Marc Mannes

Technically produced by
    Jacqueline F. Aguino & Pearl Atcitty

Design, layout, and production by
    C. Kinsman Design
    925 6th Street NW
    Albuquerque, NM 87102

Desktop publishing by
    Desktop Press
    324 12th Street NW
    Albuquerque, NM 87102

Printed by
    Bookcrafters
    Chelsea, Michigan

CONTENTS

ACKNOWLEDGMENTS

This publication, *Family Preservation and Indian Child Welfare*, has been developed and will be disseminated by the Diffusion Center, American Indian Law Center, Inc. (AILC), Albuquerque, New Mexico. The Diffusion Center has been established to offer policy analysis, training, and technical assistance to tribal, state, and local governments, and Native American organizations. This includes sharing successful techniques, management strategies, and promising and proven practices that improve the operation of service programs.

The editor would like to extend special thanks to all of the authors, reviewers of manuscripts, and especially the clients and professionals whose time and ideas made an immeasurable contribution to the content of this publication.

The book is the product of a grant funded by the Children's Bureau, Administration for Children, Youth and Families, Office of Human Development Services, U.S. Department of Health and Human Services.

The grant, number 90CW0900, was entitled "Project INTACT: Indian Teams Acting For Children." The opinions expressed are those of the authors and/or AILC, and should not be interpreted as necessarily reflecting the views of the federal government.

PREFACE

In 1987, the American Indian Law Center, Inc., decided to examine the potential benefit of family preservation and consider its applicability to Indian human services, as well as to encourage experimentation with the concept. The Law Center received a two-year national demonstration grant from the federal Children's Bureau to administer an effort entitled Project INTACT. Project INTACT was designed to help promote and facilitate the development of family preservation models and projects within tribal government agencies and Indian nonprofit organizations, identify factors that must be dealt with to establish family preservation services, begin to assess the effectiveness of new and existing efforts, and promote and coordinate information pooling and exchange among existing American Indian and Alaskan Native programs. This publication is a product of Project INTACT and a result of exploring the appropriateness of family preservation for Indian people.

Putting together a publication on the implications of family preservation for Indian human services is fraught with a number of complications. To begin with, clarifying what family preservation means presents a formidable challenge. Multiple definitions and manifold perspectives coexist and have to be reconciled. This publication chooses to conceive of family preservation in relatively broad terms and views it as a concept encompassing service programs that are family oriented and provide services in the home in order to prevent the placement of children in substitute care.

The current fanfare surrounding family preservation must also be taken into consideration. Family preservation is a "hot" concept, and is viewed by many as the "raging fad" in child welfare and across the human services. This status, though, entails certain liabilities. While proponents view it as a concept and mode of thinking that strikes a most responsive chord and details a whole new and improved way of doing business, detractors can argue that family preservation is just a passing fancy soon to be replaced by yet another newfangled idea.

A prime dilemma with anything that is new and in vogue is whether it should only be a fad or if it deserves to be more than a fad. For Indian programs, these matters take on an even greater meaning. Indian programs must strike a balance between honoring the uniquely "Indian" features of their environment (and running the risk of isolation from the field) and keeping abreast of new developments in the field (and running the risk of being swept along with each new fad).

Beyond more immediate concerns with the effectiveness and success of family preservation programs, there are a number of pertinent questions that could help determine the long-term value and viability of family preservation: Does family preservation uncover some critical truths about serving children and families that have been lost or gone unnoticed over time? Can family preservation serve as the catalyst to reorient politicians', diverse professional communities', and the general public's thinking and contribute to restructuring a badly fragmented service delivery system? Does family preservation reflect a paradigm shift in the way this society will chose to deal with families and children in need? Is family preservation nothing more than a new revenue source that could be called anything and is being embraced by professionals as a means of bailing out a service system that has been cruelly and systematically underfunded for a number of years?

Early returns from evaluation studies are being compiled and analyzed and will help answer the effectiveness question. At this time, responses to the more long-range queries are rudimentary and in short supply. Greater insights will only come about through more extensive employment of and experiences with family preservation services.

After numerous presentations and discussions at Indian conferences and meetings and countless conversations with tribal elected officials, practitioners, and administrators in Indian settings, there is reason to believe that beyond the hoopla and the pizzazz surrounding the concept, and even though answers to many critical questions are far from conclusive, family preservation holds enormous potential for American Indians and Alaskan Natives. It brings to the agenda some very important matters that many Indian communities must confront and offers some novel ways of conceptualizing and responding to the needs of many Indian children and families.

This collection of five articles implores the reader to consider the merits of family preservation and its relevance to Indian child welfare. Each offers a different vantage point on and highlights a critical facet of family preservation. Cumulatively, they move from the inception of services through the evaluation of their effectiveness. Since family preservation represents not just a way of delivering services but also a way of thinking, most of the articles incorporate some philosophic underpinnings of the approach.

The first article serves as an introduction and presents a brief historical account of the evolution of family-oriented services, a contemporary context for understanding the emergence of family preservation along with its current application, and an analysis of its relevance to Indian people. Questions to which each Native American and Alaskan Native community must seek answers are posed. The second article deals with the topic of implementation and considers the issues that need to be dealt with in order to implement family preservation services. The third explores clinical and treatment issues central to the delivery of home-based and family-centered therapy. The fourth discusses the attitudes and skills workers need in order to provide family preservation services. The fifth essay deals with the topic of evaluation and how to go about developing and managing family preservation services with evaluation in mind.

This volume has been produced for people interested in how family preservation may be utilized by American Indians and Alaskan Natives. It is written for elected officials, policy makers, judges, and service providers who are intent upon or are considering establishing a family preservation program and could use assistance in deciding how to proceed and what to do. The volume can also serve as a suitable educational resource, such as a set of supplemental readings, for students in human service and social work education programs.

I sincerely hope all readers find that the essays challenge their assumptions and perceptions of the status quo and stimulate creative thoughts about how things might be changed for the better.

Marc Mannes, Director, Project INTACT
American Indian Law Center, Inc.

Linking Family Preservation and Indian Child Welfare: A Historical Perspective and the Contemporary Context[*]

MARC MANNES

INTRODUCTION

Family preservation has emerged as a galvanizing concept in family and children's services. Family preservation is an expansive concept that incorporates: 1) core philosophic tenets enjoining society to recognize that every child should grow up in a permanent family and proposing that the best way to accomplish permanency is by preserving families and preventing the placement of children outside the home, 2) a set of action theories prescribing how service agencies should respond to children and families in need, and 3) a portfolio of practice technologies promoting the usage of specific service delivery techniques and interventions.

This article discusses all three aspects of family preservation and addresses some of the issues raised by applying it to Indian Child Welfare. The first part briefly views the contemporary emergence of family preservation as part of a larger political and social policy movement extending beyond child welfare, and examines the historic roots of family preservation in relation to American society's responses to children and families in need. General information about family preservation is introduced, including where the origins of the concept lie, some sense of how it has evolved, what the term has come to mean, and how it is currently being employed. This background is essential to understanding and determining the suitability of family preservation for Indian programs.

The second part considers the application of the concept of family

* The author would like to thank Philip S. Deloria, Bettie Rushing, and Ying-Ying T. Yuan for their review and critique of earlier versions of this essay.

1

preservation to Indian people and Indian Child Welfare. This requires reflecting on policy and programmatic development during the first decade of implementation of the Indian Child Welfare Act. An interpretation of the emphasis of Indian Child Welfare during that decade, an analysis of where Indian Child Welfare is at this point , and an assessment of the value family preservation holds for Indian Child Welfare are all highlighted. Examples of several program efforts in family preservation operated by tribal government agencies and Indian nonprofits, and some preliminary insights from these programs are reviewed.

In ascertaining the possible role for family preservation with American Indians and Alaskan Natives and what that role might be, some specific cultural and historical concerns require review. The most basic is, unquestionably, an examination of the forces prompting shifts in family functions over time and the consequences of those on the family. Still another is the potential effect of family preservation on current policies and the present status and capabilities of programs responding to the needs of Indian children and families.

Thorough examination of all of these issues cannot be fully addressed in this brief introductory article, but even this short presentation will help orient the reader and give resonance to many of the articles that follow in this collection.

UNDERSTANDING WHAT IS MEANT BY FAMILY PRESERVATION

The Recent Emphasis on the Family in Public Policy

Diamond (1983) traces contemporary political interest in the family to Jimmy Carter's presidency. During his administration, Mr. Carter convened a White House conference on the family and even appointed a special adviser on family policy.

Why was this emphasis on the family suddenly thrust into the spotlight? Consistent with Stern's (1984) definition of "administrative politics," it reflected efforts by a number of groups to continue the expansion of social welfare activities in a very specific manner. According to Diamond (1983), members of Congress, opinion leaders, intellectuals, social welfare advocates, and bureaucrats searching for ways to assist children mutually reoriented their thinking and analysis and settled on the family as the basis for improving the lot of children. The renaming of the old Department of Health, Education, and Welfare's Office of Child Development as the Administration for Children, Youth,

2

and Families at the very beginning of the Carter administration was emblematic of this new perspective.

Interest, though, was not limited only to families in need. Throughout the 1980s, the family was the recipient of attention from politicians at all levels of government. Legislation touted as supporting the family was regularly introduced and lauded at the national level throughout the decade, and the idea of supporting the family became one of the few available issues for politicians from across the political spectrum to rally around.

While liberal and conservative, progressive and reactionary seemed to agree the family was a worthwhile notion to support, the variety of means advocated to render assistance showed how differently family support could be defined and legislated. The many and diverse family-oriented initiatives have sought economic, political, and social ends. Upon closer inspection, the "family political agenda" has generally consisted of a mix of initiatives aimed at diverse classes and special groups and quite often contained an implicit ideological perspective. Several examples will reveal the array of initiatives under the umbrella of family policy.

For the middle class and the working poor, pronounced support existed for child care programs for dual paycheck families, with disagreement over whether the government should manage the services or whether parents should receive tax breaks and seek their own provider. For families with special needs children, the 1986 Amendments to the Education for All Handicapped Children, Public Law 99-457, established the Individualized Family Service Plan (IFSP). The IFSP signaled a departure from previous legislation in that the family, and not the child, is viewed as the recipient of services; and assessments of the needs of the entire family must be made. Also, family participation in the decision-making process about what services should be provided is mandated (Krauss 1990). For the poor, undereducated, and unskilled young mother, various reform packages have been developed to ease her and her progeny off welfare dependency and into employment opportunities where she'll be depositing money into the public coffers as a result of taxation rather than withdrawing it by way of public assistance.

This emphasis on the family has found expression in child welfare. A significant number of efforts underway to preserve the family unit and prevent the placement of children in substitute care have come to be known as family preservation services (FPS). They are a result of a surge of interest in how public child welfare agencies are responding to children and families in need. FPS target situations where a child is at risk

3

of being removed from the home because of abusive and/or negligent behaviors on the part of parents. Family preservation services are also offered by other public agencies concerned with children and youth. Programs designed to prevent out-of-home placements are provided for status offenders being processed through the juvenile justice system and for emotionally and behaviorally disturbed children being treated in the mental health arena.

The Antecedents of Family Preservation

While the intrinsic merit of the philosophic premises and practices underlying family preservation services now appear patently obvious, it has not always been so. The lavish attention being bestowed upon FPS can better be appreciated after briefly reviewing how American society's responses to families and children in need have varied over time.

An ever-changing mix of social moods, economic forces, legislative enactments, and political movements during particular time periods have defined what is unacceptable family behavior, identified the aspects of family problems to be addressed, and shaped the form and substance of society's interventions. Decisions about the types of approaches most suitable and valid for responding to the needs of families have in large part been based upon changing determinations about who within the family is singled out as the source of the problem.

Gordon (1988) identifies several major phases in her historical analysis of America's response to problems or violence in the family: 1) the child-saving period from 1875 to 1910, 2) the progressive era and its aftermath from 1910 to 1930, 3) the Depression from 1930 to 1940, 4) World War II and the 1950s, and 5) the 1960s and 1970s.

The first phase of involvement was triggered by the social and economic problems precipitated by skyrocketing immigration and the dizzying pace of urbanization during the second half of the nineteenth century (McGowan 1988). An emergent bourgeois class was concerned with what they perceived as "aberrant" family behaviors engaged in by many immigrant families, and the large numbers of children and young adults who roamed the streets of numerous big cities, many of whom engaged in criminal acts. The immediate response was to establish state and local institutions to care for dependent, orphaned, and wayward young people (Rothman 1980). As the horrors of warehousing the abandoned and delinquent in institutions were repeatedly exposed, a number of private sector reforms were initiated by wealthy individuals. The concept of foster homes was devised as an alternative to institution-

4

alization, charitable societies were developed and staffed by volunteers who went into homes and worked with parents, and organizations were established to protect children from parental cruelty. Gordon (1988) points out that interventions with problem families focused on preventing acts of cruelty and abuse, including such acts as incest and wife-beating. These interventions targeted the father, or male, in the household and, consistent with the anti-temperance movement, focused on excessive alcohol usage. The goal was to reform the male through punishment and/or moralizing and, if that failed, to remove the children from the home and prevent them from being subjected to additional abuse. Also during this phase, paltry sums of public financial assistance were provided to families mired in poverty; states, counties, and townships provided funds to impoverished families in their homes under a system known as "out-door relief" (Warner, Queen & Harper 1930).

The second phase was marked by the gradual emergence of federal intervention in the lives of families. A White House Conference on Children held in 1909 supported the notion of keeping dependent children with their families and only removing them as a last resort. The creation of the Children's Bureau in 1912 formally established federal involvement on behalf of children. With the passage of the Sheppard-Towner Act in 1921, the Children's Bureau had the authority to provide grants to states for maternal and child health care. A protracted battle over whether financial aid to families should be rendered by private charity or public assistance was finally won by the public advocates, over the opposition of many early leaders of the social work profession, and brought about through the passage of mothers' pension laws in most states (McGowan 1988). During this second phase, society's concern shifted from abuse to neglect; and interventions focused not on the abusive father but on the negligent mother. Gordon (1988) intimates this was probably in response to the large number of single-parent families headed by women that lived in poverty conditions and were likely to come into contact with child welfare agencies. Gordon goes on to assert that forms of family violence such as wife-beating and incest were generally overlooked by authorities and not responded to, and girls were held accountable for any assaults that took place and blamed for being sexually delinquent.

Against this backdrop, the intent and purpose of family services was becoming increasingly clouded. Public family welfare work had always primarily involved providing cash subsidies to pauper families through outdoor relief departments or mothers' pension bureaus. Private agencies performing family work included societies that grew out of old

5

charity organization societies and sectarian Catholic and Jewish entities. Their goal was to "build character" and establish "family solidarity" (Witmer 1942). Over time, formally educated social workers gradually replaced the wealthy ladies that had traditionally staffed the private agencies and brought with them subspecialties in child welfare such as school social work and courts and correctional social work. As a result, family-oriented work became increasingly marginal and was forced to rethink its purpose. According to Richmond (1922), family social work was confronted with several choices. It could 1) decide it consisted of whatever remained after the specialties have done their work, 2) make the family worker the *general practitioner* [emphasis added] of the social service field, or 3) redefine family work as a specialty with a precise function.

During the third phase, federal government involvement in the affairs of children and families was solidified by way of Titles IV and V of the Social Security of 1935. This established the forerunner of what is now known as Aid To Families With Dependent Children (AFDC) and provided funds for states to establish children's services and effectively manage those services. In retrospect, the Act's separation of administrative responsibilities for these two efforts solidified services into two distinct camps. On the one hand there were child welfare programs operated by the Children's Bureau, while on the other hand there was public financial assistance managed by the Social Security Board and later the Board of Public Assistance. The painful irony is that even though it has always been obvious that a large portion of the foster care population overlapped the public assistance caseload, statutes, regulations, and practices prevented the two arenas from being linked and services from being integrated (Kamerman & Kahn 1989). This schism helped suppress the formation of public family-oriented services.

In terms of social work's responses to problem families, male violence continued to be de-emphasized; and when it had to be acknowledged, it was quickly rationalized as an expression of stress emanating from the Depression and male unemployment (Gordon 1988). At the same time, social workers failed to demonstrate sensitivity to the plight of mothers often forced to find work outside of the home while retaining full responsibility for maintaining their families. Social workers held mothers responsible for creating and sustaining the mood of the family; and where there were outbreaks of discord and violence, reconciliation was promoted (Gordon 1988).

Through World War II, and increasingly in the 1950s, the emphasis of interventions shifted more toward psychological services. Dysfunctions

6

within families were assessed and interpreted from a psychological perspective, with the problems seen as stemming from individual complexes and inadequacies and not as a result of economic, political, or social factors. Mothers again found themselves held accountable for instances of abuse. Child abuse was seen not as a result of poverty but as a consequence of psychological rejection and associated forms of emotional neglect (Gordon 1988). From a service delivery perspective public child welfare services had grown increasingly divorced from voluntary family services, and there were virtually no public family services available (McGowan 1988).

According to Gordon, during the 1960s and 1970s attention had moved beyond a singular concentration on motherly neglect and expanded to additionally deal with wife-beating and incest issues. Moreover, throughout the 1960s, social, economic, and political issues were often incorporated into the analysis of and response to family dysfunctions; and psychological assessments and psychodynamic treatment strategies became a standard part of the treatment regimen prescribed for families.

The Emergence of Family Preservation Within Child Welfare

The stimulus for current interest in family preservation in child welfare can in large part be traced to the Adoption Assistance and Child Welfare Act of 1980, Public Law 96-272, which was passed to alter the way in which the public child welfare system was serving dependent children suffering from abuse and neglect. The law was designed to support and preserve the integrity of families, reduce the number of children "drifting" in the foster care system, set guidelines for permanency planning, and reverse federal financial incentives which had made foster care placement an immediate and seemingly advantageous choice when deciding how to respond to abuse and neglect cases. The law sought to keep families intact by preventing the unnecessary separation of children from their parents, and emphasized the importance of providing services to support and strengthen families in an attempt to avoid removing the child and placing him or her in substitute care.

Since the passage of P.L. 96-272, the federal government has acted to promote the implementation of policies and procedures to meet the legislation's intent; and numerous states and other jurisdictions have sought to comply and embarked on efforts to reduce the number of children in placement by in part striving to preserve families. A number

7

of these activities will be discussed later in this article.

In truth, work with families to prevent out-of-home placement, and the elements of what has became FPS, existed prior to the passage of P.L. 96-272. During the 1970s, an increasing number of programs had sprung up around the country which sought to work , in an intensive way and in their own homes, with families experiencing an economic, emotional, or social crisis in order to preserve the family unit. This service orientation coincided with several related trends that mutually reinforced the emphasis on families.

First, it converged with a growing awareness and acceptance within the helping professions of viewing families as systems and with the more widespread employment of specific family-based therapeutic and counseling techniques. In the mental health field, Pasamanick, Scarpitti, and Dinitz (1967) showed that short-term, in-home therapy with families that wanted members hospitalized minimized the need for hospitalization and linked the family to other services they needed. According to Hinckley and Ellis (1985), Pavenstedt (1967) demonstrated the importance of involving the entire family system when working with multi-problem families; and various practitioners such as Bellack & Small (1965) and Mann (1973) showed the effectiveness of short-term and focused therapy with outpatients. In the social services, a small number of primarily private providers transferred these principles in working with families at risk to try to prevent placement (Hutchinson & Nelson 1985).

Second, it paralleled a rising concern among advocates, child welfare professionals, and clients over what appeared to be a pattern of unnecessary and excessive placement of children in substitute care, the failure to provide appropriate services to children while in placement, and the seeming inability to quickly return children in placement to their biological families or have them adopted (McGowan 1988).

Heightened interest and attention from public legislative and executive agency officials at federal and state levels during the 1980s were grounded more in fiscal realities. The AFDC Foster Care Amendment, passed by Congress in 1971, had authorized open-ended federal matching funds to states to care for children from families eligible for AFDC who are placed in foster care as a result of judicial determination of need. Many states approved similar funding mechanisms in order to be consistent with the federal provision. A concern for the inability to reduce the number of children in substitute care, and the increasing outlays required to support that population in placement, motivated the search for alternative responses to families in crisis and children at risk.

Private philanthropy also played an important role in popularizing the concept of family preservation throughout the decade of the 1980s. The Edna McConnell Clark Foundation directed a large portion of its financial resources to advocate for family preservation at the state and local level, provide seed money for the start-up of new programs, disseminate instructional materials describing how to apply the concept, and train direct service and management staff in administrative and practice techniques (Nelson 1988).

Describing Family Preservation Programs

As an evolving concept receiving an overwhelming amount of attention, family preservation remains open to much interpretation. In order to provide some sense of its current application and help readers appreciate where the field is, this article will make use of the standards set for services to strengthen and preserve families with children that were recently published by the Child Welfare League of America (CWLA 1989).

The standards distinguish among three different models of family preservation programs that can be seen as falling along a continuum of services to families with children. The first model is labeled Family Resource, Support, And Education Services (FRSE). FRSE are defined as "community-based services that assist and support adults in their role as parents, with the primary objectives of promoting parental competencies and behaviors that lead to healthy and positive personal development of both children and their parents" (CWLA 1989, p.13). This type of service program is provided to families that are perceived as being in need of assistance and is delivered via community drop-in centers or in the home of the family. The overall goal is to help mothers and fathers become more effective parents.

The second model is Family-Centered Services (FC). According to CWLA (1989), FC Services "encompass a range of activities for families with problems that threaten their stability: case management, counseling/therapy, education/skill building, advocacy, and/or the provision of concrete services such as food, housing, or health care" (p. 29). They are designed to protect the safety and wellbeing of children, as well as stabilize families. They are initiated in response to a child or parent(s) requesting assistance, or to a referral.

The third model of family preservation service is known as Intensive Family-Centered Crisis (IFC) Services. IFC services respond to families in crisis and are employed "at a time when removal of a child from the

9

home is imminent, or the return of a child from out-of-home care is being considered" (CWLA 1989, p. 46). IFC services share characteristics with the other types of family preservation programs: they are typically provided in the home of the family, and a mixture of services is provided. In contrast to the other types, IFC service programs are particularly time-limited and intensive. Services are offered for a specific duration such as four to six weeks or 90 days. During this short time frame, workers serve a limited number of families and spend a lot of time with each. In general, the programs which serve families for a shorter period of time provide more hours of service per week. For example, a six-week program might provide ten to fifteen hours of service per week per family, whereas a three-month program would provide fewer hours of service. Caseload size also tends to vary with the length of service. The shorter programs usually maintain two or three families per worker. Often each family is served by a team consisting of two workers.

Currently, many people in the field use the term "family preservation" exclusively in relation to the IFC model. In addition, IFC services are currently most frequently offered and therefore receive more attention. This article, however, uses family preservation in a broader sense and as an umbrella term covering all three models of service programs, although the emphasis of the discussion is on the FC and IFC models.

While certainly quite different in terms of design and delivery, all three types of family preservation services share a common goal. They ascribe to the theory that most young peoples' needs are best met by remaining with their natural families, and that by helping parents to more effectively function as caregivers and childrearers, family and community life can be enhanced.

CONSIDERING FAMILY PRESERVATION IN RELATION TO INDIAN CHILD WELFARE

Making the Case for the Relevance of Family Preservation to Indian Child Welfare

Advocates for Indian children have long held concerns that the number of Native children in substitute care is persistently and extremely high, the percentage in care remains much greater than for other groups of children, and insufficient efforts are being made to prevent the out-of-home placement of American Indian and Alaskan Native children.

A federally funded study of Indian child welfare (Plantz et al. 1988) has confirmed these concerns and found, disturbingly, that despite the passage of the Indian Child Welfare Act (ICWA) the number of Indian children in care has risen from about 7,200 in the early 1980s to 9,005 in 1986. Not only has the ICWA not stemmed the tide but the number of Indian children in placement has apparently increased approximately 25% during the decade of the 1980s. Although Indian children make up 0.9% of the total child population in the United States, they represent 3.1% of the total substitute care population. They are placed in substitute care at a rate that is 3.6 times greater than the rate for non-Native children.

Moreover, there was widespread evidence to confirm a lack of placement prevention services. The study could only document preventive efforts in 41% of a sample of case records reviewed for Native children in public agency care, 37% of a sample of case records reviewed for children under tribal government agency care, and 33% of a sample of case records reviewed for Native children in Bureau of Indian Affairs care.

Family problems contributing to the potential placement of Indian children in substitute care must be taken into consideration. According to the Milwaukee Indian Health Board, Inc. (1987), some of the more general problems Indian families confront are: 1) perpetuating cycles of violence, 2) social isolation in both urban and rural environments, 3) economic deprivation, 4) poor child-rearing skills, 5) personal frustration, 6) guilt, 7) emotional trauma, 8) marital problems, 9) too many children, 10) rigid sex roles, 11) drug and alcohol consumption, 12) psychoses, and 13) poor health. The results of a major study of abuse and neglect patterns among the Navajo showed such cases tended to emerge from larger families whose adult members were unemployed and supported by public funds (White & Cornely 1981).

The Plantz et al. study (1988) revealed the distribution of reasons prompting the placement of Indian children. In its review and comparison of tribal, public, BIA, and off-reservation child welfare programs, the study found that roughly 78% of Indian children were placed because of parental behavior or problems. The multiple reasons behind parental-induced placements can be organized into a protective services category including abuse and neglect, and an additional parental problems category including substance abuse, abandonment, and hardship. Parental instances of abuse and neglect appeared to account for about 50% of the total 78% with the additional category of parental problems making up the remaining 28%. The 50% of placements attributed to abuse and neglect comprised, on average, 37% neglect and 13% abuse. Approximately half of the 28% of placements resulting from additional parental problems—roughly 14%—were a result of parental substance abuse.

11

Hardship, abandonment, and other parental problems combined to make up the remaining 14% in the additional parental problems category. Also, the study data led its authors to believe substance abuse played a major role in many of the neglect-related placements.

These findings clarify why placements occur and provide a compelling argument that interventions to preserve and strengthen families and reduce out-of-home placements are needed within Indian Child Welfare.

The Emphasis on Placement in the Evolution of Indian Child Welfare

The results of the Plantz et al. study are not surprising when one realizes virtually all programmatic developments and legal battles throughout the first decade of the ICWA's existence have almost exclusively dealt with placement-related concerns.

The dilemma in all of child welfare is based upon seeking a balance between protecting children and preserving families. The emphasis on placement during the first ten years of the ICWA is a reflection of practitioners making the protection of children paramount. This emphasis on placement and child protection is probably in part intentional and in part a result of circumstances. Perhaps the emphasis is tied to the fact that issues of placement brought the ICWA into existence.

Anguish and anger surrounding placement catalyzed the original drafting and passage of the Indian Child Welfare Act. The placement of Indian children with non-Indian families and the specter of how that practice fostered a form of cultural genocide was used to justify the passage of the ICWA.

During the past ten years Indian and other social service professionals have struggled to find sufficient numbers of Indian foster homes and quality Indian foster parents in response to the growing need for placements. A large number of tribal and nonprofit Indian Child Welfare programs have chosen to remove children from troubled families and send them to live with aunts and uncles or grandparents. These "relative placements" are viewed by the non-Indian child welfare system as temporary or long-term foster care settings. Thus, tribal governments and Indian nonprofits rendering children and family services have had to fight with states and force them to accept extended family placements as legitimate. Indian Child Welfare programs have had to develop placement standards that are culturally appropriate, honest, and true to unique tribal traditions. Once developed, Indian Child Welfare programs have had to battle with states to get them to accept the placement

12

standards. Also, program personnel have labored to find sensitive and caring institutional settings where troubled youngsters can be placed and healed.

Administrative and funding factors have also contributed to this emphasis on placement. Over the years the Bureau of Indian Affairs, the main source of Indian Child Welfare funds, has sanctioned primarily child protection and placement-related ventures and only recently has begun to urge those seeking funds to address family-oriented preventive services.

Another explanation for tribal social services and Indian nonprofits not providing placement prevention services and family-oriented services, when family focused work is so congruent with traditions, may be due to limited resources. A constant shortage of funds, staff, and capabilities have no doubt prevented the establishment of comprehensive service systems that work with children, parents, and families. The shifting and ephemeral nature of federal policies, program priorities, and appropriations has undermined the formation of service delivery infrastructures. Appropriations since the passage of the ICWA have been inconsistent and inadequate. By and large, tribes and nonprofit Indian agencies offering child welfare services have been forced to battle one another in annual or biennial discretionary grant competition. As a result, the scope of children's and family services has fluctuated wildly; and programs often just disappear when a grant proposal is not funded. In the absence of consistent programming and levels of support, an almost exclusive reliance on grantsmanship and advocacy has led to the creation of hodgepodge and makeshift "systems" dependent upon funding streams, program availability, and political maneuvering. Tribes and nonprofits have been forced to establish services based on categorical grants and discretionary funding sources while other jurisdictions build services on block grants and entitlement funding (Mannes 1990).

The Consequences of Emphasizing Placement

The emphasis on placement during the first ten years of the ICWA is a by-product of limited resources being used by those in the field to primarily protect and respond to the needs of children. This emphasis on placement has not been wrong or inappropriate; it was and will continue to be necessary and essential. More importantly, placement-related efforts to ensure the security and safety of young people should not be abated.

At the same time, however, a singleminded and exclusive focus on placement is ultimately too limiting. The centrality of placement has contributed to a narrowing of the perceptions of how workers view their work world and what they attend to, and has limited the definitions of what workers see as important and the work they actually perform. Pecora et al. (1985), stress how worker attitudes and practices probably need to undergo changes if family-centered services are to succeed.

The continuing emphasis on placement is contributing tragically to the creation of yet another generation of American Indians and Alaskan Natives who are not going to be able to maintain families and raise their children. Initially, the major federal policy of assimilation and its related sub-policies, such as compulsory education that ushered in boarding schools, forced the removal of Indian children from their families in order to inculcate them in the ways of American society. This severed family relations and prevented a generation of Indian adults from being able to raise their children. Next, the actions of state, county, and local social services removed Indian children from their families and helped create another generation of Indians unable to maintain families and raise their offspring.

This pattern seems to be continuing, with an unlikely source—namely tribes—apparently perpetuating it. One of the most startling findings of the Plantz et al. study cited earlier was the indication that tribally run Indian Child Welfare programs appear to be the primary contributor to the increasing rate of placement. The ICWA reaffirmed the inherent power of tribal governments over their young people, set forth procedures for the tribal reassumption of responsibility for their young through the transfer of jurisdiction, and acknowledged the powers of tribes to intervene into the affairs of families. The Plantz et al. study data leads one to infer that the ICWA works and that tribes are assuming responsibility for more and more of their children as states recede from the picture. The data also seems to suggest that tribally based child welfare projects are responding to the resulting increases in caseloads by behaving similarly to other jurisdictional units and making extensive use of placement.

It may seem provocative to suggest that this continuing emphasis on placement, the implications of which are not yet widely or clearly recognized, is contributing to the breakup of families and preventing a number of adults from being able to keep and raise their children; but that may just be the case. Attempts must be made to respond to this problem, and family preservation offers the hope and the potential to do that.

The Implications of Moving beyond Placement and Applying Family Preservation to Indian Child Welfare

Introducing the concept of family preservation implores all who are concerned with Indian Child Welfare to stop, pause, and give some thought to what has been dealt with since the passage of the ICWA. The concept of family preservation entails a philosophy and maintains a program orientation which has the potential to broaden Indian Child Welfare's vision of its mission.

At the very least, family preservation asks that some attention, thought, and action should be shifted from placement to placement prevention with an emphasis on the family. At most, it is quite possible that family preservation services offer the next major challenge for those who work with troubled Indian children and families.

In considering the application of family preservation to Indian Child Welfare, a major issue will be to determine not only how to expand or reorient in order to serve, strengthen, and heal families, but also how to resolve the fundamental tension between protecting children via placements and keeping families intact.

Embracing family preservation will raise the stakes for Indian Child Welfare programs, along with all other Indian social service programs and the clients they work with. With family preservation, the concern becomes one of responding not just to the needs of at-risk children and youth, but also to the needs of troubled adults who are the parents of troubled, abused, and neglected children and youth. For, in the long run, there can never be real hope to transform troubled, multiproblem, dysfunctional families into functional families by removing the children and doing very little for the parents. In some cases removal may be necessary. In fact, in certain instances a parent may request a placement. Yet, the assumption of family preservation is that placements will be carried out only after the rights and privacy of parents have been weighted against protecting the child and efforts have been undertaken to prevent placement.

The introduction of family preservation may force Indian service providers to reconceptualize and restructure their services to the community. Even though welfare, mental health, and child welfare are funded independently and from different sources, they may have to be implemented in tandem.

The initiation of family preservation services presents the additional challenge of figuring out how to identify, assess, and intervene effectively with families in need; because removal of children from the home is increasingly being recognized as only a temporary solution—a type of social bandage. Why bandage? Because the wounds may be covered through placement, but nothing is done to heal the wounds causing placement. In far too many cases, children placed in substitute care eventually wind up returning to a troubled home; and troubled parents wind up having more children for whom human services eventually inherit responsibility.

Besides, placing children does not seem to have resolved difficulties. Tribal and urban Indian human service providers repeatedly lament that it is the adults who spent much of their childhood in substitute care, of whatever form, who are now establishing a new wave of troubled families, producing a new generation of troubled children, and forcing child welfare programs to deal with the issue of placing their children in substitute care.

In addition, with placement rates so high, family preservation can be used as a strategy for reunification. Several agencies are in fact using FPS to bring families back together.

Another aspect that cannot be overlooked in providing services is the social context within which families operate. As Anderson (1982) makes clear, degrees of support, feedback, and connectedness with one's community can contribute immensely to adaptive and maladaptive family behaviors and patterns. Families have specific social transactions with other families that lead to the formation of social bonds and social networks. These networks and bonds facilitate the exchange of essential information, provide concrete services, render support, and offer companionship; they lead to positive benefits like promoting security, connectedness, and belonging. This assumes, of course, that the shared and interactive behaviors are healthy and productive.

But, what happens when the social networks and bonds are built on activities that are destructive and dysfunctional? Alcoholism serves as the prime example. Those who work with Indian families know of the extreme social and peer pressure often placed on family members to drink. With this in mind, it is not surprising that at least one tribe has wanted to work simultaneously with multiple families where alcohol is a problem for the purpose of having a network of families who have gone through recovery together and can support one another and help withstand community pressures to resume alcohol consumption. It is worth considering that the success certain Indian communities have had in combatting alcoholism is a result of making the efforts community wide and transforming the social norms and network to one that sweepingly deplores the use of alcohol and establishes bonds to reinforce the principle.

Somehow and in some way, Indian Child Welfare and Indian social and mental health projects need to begin to find a coordinated way to deal with families; because troubled children most often come from troubled families, and troubled families help to sustain troubled communities. Solutions will not come easy and the price tag will not come cheap. Whether there is the political will and the professional commitment to come up with answers is still to be seen. The support of workers will be easier to secure than political patronage, but the effort to accomplish both will take time.

Coming to Terms with the Concept of Family

Family preservation requires coming to a more lucid understanding of what families represent and what they are supposed to accomplish. Coontz (1988) views the family as the concrete expression of a socially sanctioned relationship between biological and social reproduction. Families operate as systems within which social relations are taught and social and biological reproduction is practiced. Social relations acquired within the family system shape attitudes and mold behaviors with regard to biological reproduction, economic production, and psychodynamics. The psychodynamic aspect influences interpersonal activities among family members, the internal psychic world of each family member, and how all family members interact with the external world and other people. In other words, the family plays as critical a role in helping shape and mediate people's definitions of themselves as individuals, socializing youngsters into the culture they're born into, and defining young people's eventual place in the social order, as it does in perpetuating the existence of a particular human group.

While the purpose of families remains constant, their functions, characteristics, and dynamics are open to change. According to Gordon (1988), changes in the form, size, and interpersonal relationship among members of a family over the course of history are in large part the result of alterations in class dynamics, ecological changes, cultural adaptations, economic transitions, and political associations.

Certain historians of the family such as Thompson (1977) argue that family relations are primarily tied to the prevailing economic system and resultant structures of work in a particular social order. Tilly and Scott (1978) pinpoint three distinct phases in the economic evolution of families and the corresponding sanctioned family form for each phase: 1) the pre-industrial economy based upon all members of the family having specific responsibilities tied to a system of household production, 2) the

17

wage economy, initially based primarily upon members of the family unit exchanging labor for wages as the market economy emerged, and over time in response to social reform movements shifting to only the male household head collecting sufficient wages to maintain a family, and 3) the consumer economy—coupled with the advent of mass production and mass consumption—in which family members focus on production and consumption rather than wages, wives are employed, and children—originally kept out of the workforce—are eventually brought back in so they too can produce and consume. Considering these ideas in relation to American Indian and Alaskan Native families will point out significant historical differences that have a bearing on Native families' present status and condition.

According to Coontz (1988), traditional methods of social relations encompassing political and economic activities within Indian societies were vastly different from those practiced by Europeans arriving in the New World. While Europeans had the private ownership of land and resources serving as the basis for social and economic relations, many Native Americans used kinship ties based upon clan relations or other traditional group orientations as the basis for establishing social obligations and responsibilities and moving goods and services over space and time. With no private ownership of land and with survival based upon sharing and reciprocity, there was no permanent labor force. No one had to trade labor for access to the basic human needs of food, clothing, and shelter. Sharing rather than accumulation of wealth served as the major source of social prestige. Leaders exhibited generosity and derived their leadership from sharing what they had with others.

Lacking the political infrastructure found in a centralized state system, Indians relied upon traditional family systems to regulate interpersonal behavior and resolve disputes and conflicts. Within the larger system of extended group relations, the family served to circulate people and resources and supported a system whereby all individuals had the means to call upon the labor and products of others. The reliance upon others implicit in the traditional family system meant Indian people had much less economic autonomy than Europeans; in contrast, the lack of an all-encompassing state apparatus meant that they had more political autonomy. Any potential destabilizing effect of political autonomy was mitigated by the overriding economic interdependencies fostered by kinship or other similar systems.

Ongoing contact and interaction with European settlers, however, had profound consequences upon traditional patterns of family relations. The modes of economic production and exchange and social reproduction between pre-colonial and colonial society and Indian society were so radically different as to throw traditional practices into disarray and to effectively undermine the continuity and utility of kinship and other indigenous family systems.

The significant metamorphosis America went through during the Jacksonian Democracy period exacerbated this alienation. During the period 1825-1850, America made the transformation from a system in which the family served as the basic unit of social and economic relations to the market system (Rogin 1976). In economics, the family no longer served as the basic unit of production. In the social sector, the family no longer performed the caretaker functions it had conducted during colonial times. The family was no longer obligated to help the orphan, the delinquent, the pauper, and the insane. Instead, those caretaker responsibilities were transferred to a set of newly emergent institutions (Rothman 1980).

As the shift to the wage-oriented family under the market system was taking place, Indian families found their traditional family systems increasingly irreconcilable with the dominant culture's system and experienced a succession of crises. Fiercely unwilling and, by virtue of domination and subjugation, seemingly unable and often not allowed to find a way to meld its traditional practices with Western approaches, the Indian family found itself becoming less and less capable of sustaining its traditional orientation and unable to acquire the means and the support mechanisms to make the transition to any of the more modern family forms. Indian people struggled to retain a system in which families functioned as the unit of production and provided "social services"; but with the traditional family systems and the social and economic relations they fostered becoming less and less viable in the face of an all-encompassing market economy, this option became increasingly unrealistic.

As a result of Indians being expelled to remote rural and western areas and isolated far from centers of economic advancement and activity, there was little work for many male heads of household to sustain a family, much less for children to help keep the family economically solvent. Many Indian families never had the means to become successful as wage-earning families. The lack of availability of jobs and associated financial resources meant many Indians were also unable to eventually establish successful consumer families. These circumstances have continued to undermine large numbers of Indian families up to the present era.

What is most amazing is the degree of tenacity and perseverance demonstrated by Indian families in the face of these debilitating circumstances. Despite the hardships, barriers, and obstacles, traditional arrangements such as clan and kinship patterns have shown a formidable resiliency and managed to survive.

The current dilemma remains one of determining if and how it is possible to retain the power and strength of traditional family systems and how they can survive within the modern socioeconomic framework from which they have been systematically excluded. The question is not only whether Indian people can and want to adopt a family form that is effectively part traditional, part wage, and part consumer (a truly unique version of the blended family) but also will the larger society make the necessary provisions to allow such a form to exist? Any family preservation movement organized to serve Indian people must contribute to some resolution of these disparities and offer some long-awaited answers.

Federal, State, and Tribal Family Preservation Initiatives for Indian People

A number of family-centered and placement prevention projects serving Indian people have been supported by the federal government, various states, and individual tribes.

The Children's Bureau, within the Administration for Children, Youth, and Families, Office of Human Development Services, Department of Health and Human Services, has employed a number of mechanisms to foster the expansion of family preservation services. A National Resource Center on Family Based Services, located at the School of Social Work, University of Iowa, has been funded to disseminate information, offer training, provide technical assistance, and perform evaluations. From FY85 through FY88, demonstration grants were made available through the research and demonstration Coordinated Discretionary Funds Program (CDP) administered by the Office of Human Development Services. In FY85, funds were earmarked for state, county, or metropolitan public child welfare agencies to implement or improve the delivery of preplacement prevention services, and the program announcement emphasized that nonprofit organizations be established as the primary provider of the service. The announcement also specified priority would be given to jurisdictions maintaining a disproportionate number of minority children in substitute care and jurisdictions in a beginning phase of offering placement prevention services.

In the FY86 CDP announcement, the solicitation for foster care placement prevention projects found in the Federal Register on September 4,

1985, acknowledged, "organizational and administrative structures and state and local financing practices appear to be barriers in shifting service provision from child placement focused to family-centered services" (p. 35919). Applications were invited from states to implement demonstration projects and make use of effective models to overcome the barriers and fully operationalize placement prevention services. In the FY87 CDP announcement, the federal request remained essentially the same as it was in FY86, except other jurisdictional units (metropolitan areas, rural or urban counties, rural consortia, rural regional structures, etc.), in addition to states, were encouraged to apply. (The American Indian Law Center, Inc., applied and was successful in obtaining funds to operate Project INTACT under the FY87 announcement.)

Finally, in the FY88 CDP announcement, a family preservation initiative was directed towards tribal and Indian nonprofit providers of family and children's services. The initiative emphasized establishing demonstration projects that would show how to design and implement placement prevention/reunification programs for American Indian families having children in care or at risk of placement due to alcoholism or alcohol abuse by the parents. Six organizations were funded under this priority area to provide placement prevention services:

Fairbanks Native Association, Inc., in Fairbanks, Alaska
Indian Health Care Resources Center in Tulsa, Oklahoma
Confederated Tribes of Grande Ronde Community in Oregon
Mississippi Band of Choctaw Indians
Puyallup Tribe in Washington
The Comanche Tribe of Oklahoma

The Office of Human Development Services subsequently funded an evaluation of these six placement prevention and alcoholism projects. The results of the study are not yet available.

Two other service providers benefitted from Administration for Children, Youth, and Families funding and operated programs responding to the needs of families in order to reduce placement. They were Denver Indian Health and Family Services, Inc., and the Bad River Tribe of Wisconsin. The Denver project sought to identify at-risk children and families and prevent the placement of children in substitute care by coordinating mental health services for children and families at risk. When placement was made, the project sought to minimize its impact and to work on reunification possibilities. It also endeavored to foster cooperation among the multiple service providers for Indian people in an urban setting. The Bad River Tribe effort was geared toward developing a comprehensive program that would prevent child abuse and neglect and help end the dissolution of Indian families on the Bad River Reservation. The initial step involved designing and administering an assessment model to identify the at-risk population. Program services including in-home skills training in how to be an effective parent, referrals to other agencies for needed services, household management skills, and advocacy for adequate housing were all combined and targeted for the at-risk families.

Certain tribes have taken the lead in formulating and operating family preservation services and have created the opportunity to secure funding. Plagued by an extremely high rate of foster care placements, the Ute Mountain Ute Tribe requested funds from the Bureau of Indian Affairs (funds that instead would have gone to pay for children in substitute care) to implement a project to prevent out-of-home placement. Entitled Project "HOME BASE" and begun in 1987, the effort consists of four components: 1) family support workers assisting family units in need, 2) strong collaboration with the school system to identify school-related problems quickly and maintain the children in school, 3) a curriculum on how to be effective parents, and 4) a reward system for parent and child accomplishments.

Two other projects run by Indian nonprofit service organizations are being supported by states. The Minnesota Indian Women's Resource Center program has also been in operation since 1987. Funded by the State of Minnesota and Hennepin County, the program serves American Indian families with young children who are likely to be placed out of the home, or families where the children are in substitute care and there is the belief they can be returned home with appropriate services. The emphasis on reunification, as well as preventing placement, provides intensive services over an eight-to-twelve week period and responds to approximately eight families at a time. A two-member team approach is used for all families and offers both in-home and agency-based services.

The Inter-Tribal Council of Michigan, Inc., received funds via a statewide family preservation effort to reduce the Indian population in foster care. The state of Michigan adopted the widely used intensive Homebuilders Model as the mechanism to keep families together and moved to implement it statewide. The inter-tribal agency was chosen to provide services to Indian families in an area where placement rates were consistently high—the Upper Peninsula of Michigan. Services are being provided almost entirely in the homes of the families, and project workers are available to families on a 24-hour basis. Consistent with the

22

Homebuilders approach, interventions will last approximately six weeks, followed by referrals to other appropriate services.

Despite the range of difficulties faced by many of the families these programs serve, virtually all the efforts build on existing family strengths and strive to assist families in developing problem-solving skills and acquiring techniques that can help prevent the recurrence of abuse, neglect, and family conflicts.

CONCLUSION

Some Final Factors to Consider

A fundamental question posed by this article—How applicable are family preservation services for Indian people?—remains to be answered by each and every community. In the course of this discussion, it has become increasingly apparent that there are two other questions that must also be answered. First, do family preservation interventions respond to the needs of Indian families? Second, where are tribes and Indian nonprofits in terms of development and in their ability to render family preservation services? The first question considers the suitability of the intervention. The second question considers the capability of tribal governments and Indian nonprofits to offer the program.

The first question necessitates a selective review of issues raised in this paper. Remember that a large portion of the theoretical basis for family preservation services is grounded in the evolution of family-based therapeutic and counseling techniques. The Family-Centered Intensive Service approach that has come to represent the lions share of FPS programs focuses on psychological interfamilial matters while dealing only tangentially with social, political, and economic issues. These other aspects of families' problems are assumed to be handled by other agencies to which the family is referred after the intensive intervention is over and the family has been stabilized.

Certainly, there are a number of problems confronting Indian families that a psychological approach can address. (See the Tafoya article on therapeutic treatment with Indian families in this volume.) But, is that enough? It would seem that any response to problems faced by Indian families which fails to concern pervasive unemployment, widespread poverty, and isolation from economic development—in other words avoids many vital social and economic factors—cannot hope to have any meaningful impact. After all, social and economic issues, like the long-term lack of meaningful work for most Indian males at wages necessary

23

to support a family, have contributed greatly to the erosion of the Indian family system. Can psychological difficulties be concentrated on, and other socioeconomic matters relegated to secondary importance, or must an equal blend of these various orientations be created and put into practice?

Family preservation has enlightened policy makers and service providers as to how families in need can be helped. Family preservation has demonstrated the possibility of helping basically emotionally and financially stable families weather a sudden interpersonal or monetary crisis. Family preservation has also shown it has the possibility of making quick changes in families experiencing constant financial, emotional, and even drug-induced crises, in environments where the families can be rapidly referred to and benefit from any one of a number of other social services.

Can family preservation play a role in responding to families who are confronted with perpetual crises, and who live in environments where there are either overextended and/or insufficient support services? Can family preservation be responsive to the needs of Indian people living in rural areas on reservations? As of now, there is no conclusive answer to any of these questions. Perhaps the evaluation of the six federally funded projects for tribes and urban Indian organizations to attempt family preservation where alcohol abuse is present will provide some clues and insights. Only through greater experimentation and application of the concept in programs serving Indian families will answers be available. It may be that hybrid forms of service designs incorporating aspects of each FPS model will need to be devised.

Some preliminary insights have emerged from work that has already transpired in family preservation. The Inter-Tribal Council of Michigan has found that a four-to-six-week period does not allow for sufficient progress and that longer service time frames may be needed. They have been seeking funds to operate a family support project that would follow on the heels of the intensive model and render longer-term assistance to families. The Minnesota Indian Woman's Resource Center has found that the greater the strength and resilience of a tribal group's customs, practices, and language and the greater connectedness a family has with those traditions, the greater is the receptivity and responsiveness to therapeutic methods. Whether these findings are site specific or can be generalized to other locations cannot be determined at this time.

The question of capability is also vital. The next article in the volume discusses issues related to the implementation of family preservation services and focuses on tribal and nonprofit capabilities in much greater detail.

Indian Child Welfare needs to deal with family preservation head-on, and the reasons are straightforward. Family preservation calls attention to circumstances and raises powerful questions that must be addressed by all professionals and parties concerned with American Indian and Alaskan Native children, youth, adults, and families. The elusive and complex answers to be discovered are crucial to invigorating and reorienting this very important work.

REFERENCES

Anderson, C. (1982). The community connection: The impact of social networks on family and individual functioning. In F. Walsh (Ed.), *Normal family processes*. New York: The Guilford Press.

Bellack, L., & Small, L. (1965). *Emergency psychotherapy and brief psychotherapy*. New York: Grune & Stratton.

Coontz, S. (1988). *The social origins of private life: A history of American families 1600-1900*. New York: Verso.

Child Welfare League of America (1989). *Standards for services to strengthen and preserve families with children*. Washington, D.C.

Diamond, I. (1983). *Families, politics, and public policy*. New York: Longman.

Gordon, L. (1988). *Heroes of their own lives: The politics and history of family violence*. New York: Viking Penguin, Inc.

Hinckley, E.C., & Ellis, W.F. (1985). An effective alternative to residential placement: Home-based services. *Journal of Clinical Child Psychology*, 14, 3, 209-213.

Hutchinson, J.R., & Nelson, K.E. (1985). How public agencies can provide family-centered services. Social Casework: *The Journal of Contemporary Social Work*, June, 367-371.

Kamerman, S.B., & Kahn, A.J. (1989). *Social services for children, youth and families in the United States*. Connecticut: The Annie E. Casey Foundation.

Krauss, M.W. (1990). New precedent in family policy: Individualized family service plan. *Exceptional Children, 56*, 5, 388-395.

Mann, T. (1973). *Time-limited psychotherapy.* Massachusetts: Harvard University Press.

Mannes, M. (1990). The perceptions of human service workers in planning for the implementation of the family preservation services innovation in Indian child welfare settings. Unpublished Dissertation. New York: Cornell University.

McGowan, B.G. (1988). Family-based services and public-policy: Context and implications. In J.K. Whittaker, J. Kinney, E.M. Tracy, & C. Booth (Eds.), *Improving practice technologies for workers with high risk families: Lessons from the homebuilders social work education project.* Washington: Center for Social Work Research, University of Washington.

Milwaukee Indian Health Board, Inc. (1987). *Contributory factors to child abuse/neglect among Indian families.* Wisconsin.

Nelson, D. (1988). *Recognizing and realizing the potential of "family preservation."* Washington, D.C.: The Center for the Study of Social Policy.

Pasamanick, B., Scarpitti, F., & Dinitz, S. (1967). *Schizophrenics in the community.* New York: McGraw-Hill.

Pavenstedt, E. (1967). *The drifters: Children of disorganized lower class.* Massachusetts: Little, Brown and Company.

Pecora, P.J., Delewski, C.H., Booth, C., Haapala, D., & Kinney, J. (1985). Home-based, family-centered services: The impact of training on worker attitudes. *Child Welfare, 64*, 5, 529-540.

Plantz, M.C., Hubbell, R., & Dobrec, A. (1988). *Indian Child Welfare: A status report*—Final report of the survey of Indian Child Welfare and implementation of the Indian Child Welfare Act and Section 428 of the Adoption Assistance and Child Welfare Act of 1980. Washington, D.C.: CSR, Inc.

Richmond, M.E. (1922). Some relations of family casework to social progress. *Family, 3*, 99-104.

Rogin, M.P. (1975). *Fathers & children: Andrew Jackson and the subjugation of the American Indian*. New York: Vintage Books.

Rothman, D.J. (1980). *Conscience and convenience. The asylum and its alternatives in progressive America*. Massachusetts: Little, Brown and Company.

Stern, M. J. (1984). The politics of American social welfare. In F.D. Perlmutter (Ed.), *Human services at risk*. Massachusetts: Lexington Books.

Tilly, L., & Scott, J. (1978). *Women, work and family*. New York: Holt, Rinehart and Winston.

Thompson, E.P. (1977). Happy Families. *New Society, 8*, September, 499-501.

Warner, A.G., Queen, S.A., & Harper, E.B. (1930). *American charities and social work*. New York: Thomas W. Crowell Company.

White, R.B., & Cornely, D.A.(1981). Navajo child abuse and neglect study: A comparison group examination of abuse and neglect of Navajo children. *Child Abuse and Neglect, 5*, 1, 9-17.

Witmer, H.L. (1942). *Social Work*. New York: Rinehart & Company, Inc.

Implementing Family Preservation Services with American Indians and Alaskan Natives

MARC MANNES

INTRODUCTION

The first part of this article discusses the strategic and practical value of studying implementation. The second part presents a host of general and specific implementation issues that may have to be dealt with when implementing family preservation services (FPS) with American Indians and Alaskan Natives. The third part of the essay offers guidelines and suggestions on how to respond effectively to broad implementation concerns and a number of the more important implementation issues.

THE IMPORTANCE OF IMPLEMENTATION

The Relationship Between Policy and Program Implementation

Meeting policy and program objectives requires successful implementation. For Williams (1975), implementation is "the stage between a decision and operations." In the broadest sense, implementation entails putting a decision into place.

In the context of social policies and social programs, implementation involves being responsive to a policy objective by deciding to implement and establish a program. Implementation usually requires bringing about changes in behaviors and related attitudes on the part of agency staff, governing bodies, elected officials, key constituency groups, the general community, and service organizations (Mazmanian & Sabatier 1981).

In the human services, social policies and service programs work in tandem in response to social problems; typically, a policy is formulated and a distinctive service program is created to accomplish the policy.

Thus, a governmental unit develops a policy responding to the plight of homeless people and decides that the homeless must be provided with shelters and given opportunities and skills to acquire employment. In order to implement the policy, service agencies receive funds through a number of different means to implement programs providing housing and job readiness services. In many respects, the success of policy implementation remains dependent upon the effectiveness of program implementation.

While policy makers and program professionals have interrelated roles in responding to human service problems, the two groups perform in vastly different realms, remain susceptible to different pressures, tend to be guided by different standards, and adhere to divergent measures of accountability.

The loosely coupled, yet interdependent nature of the policy and program spheres serves to complicate and confound the implementation process. Anyone who has ever worked in developing social policy or in delivering human services knows how difficult and complex the implementation of policies and programs is. It is one thing for Congress, a tribal council, or board of directors to affirm and support a policy de-emphasizing the out-of-home placement of children and to establish a package of family support services. It is quite another to implement FPS to accomplish those policy goals.

In this essay, implementation will concentrate on issues that need to be contended with and concrete activities that need to be performed once either there has been a decision to implement a family preservation effort, or a particular individual, group of individuals, or a community is trying to decide whether to implement family preservation services and what will need to be dealt with.*

Implementation and Program Failure

A wealth of professional experiences and reports make it abundantly clear that the implementation of policies and programs is more susceptible to failure than to success. Why is this the case? Why is it so hard to get a policy and program off the drawing board and have it work?

Policies and programs fail for two basic reasons. The first can be labeled a "theory failure" (Weiss 1972), in which the policy and program

---

* While the emphasis in this article is on the implementation of FPS, many of the techniques discussed, issues raised, and methods suggested are relevant to the implementation of many other human service programs.

are implemented as designed and yet fail to have the intended effect. The second is a result of what is known as "program failure" (Weiss 1972), wherein the policy or program is not or cannot be implemented as it was designed. In theory failure, implementation occurred but the anticipated and desired outcomes were not attained. In program failure, certain factors or circumstances inhibited or prevented implementation from taking place.

Our understanding of program failure is quite limited because many evaluation studies are apt to focus on theory failure and ignore program failure (Patton 1986). This isn't surprising in light of Dye's (1972) reminder that governmental actions contribute to program failure as a result of an inclination to pursue incompatible goals simultaneously and a tendency to create policies and programs for little more than symbolic value. Clearly governments are not predisposed to fund studies that would highlight their contribution to program failure. As a result, effectiveness, as defined under the present system, has come to rest on assessing outcomes and analyzing the consequences or results of a particular intervention. McGowan (1988) identifies this pattern in her analysis of the relationship between family-based services and policies. She points out how evaluations have been designed to assess the effectiveness of particular practices and not to answer questions about the viability of a family-oriented policy or whether sufficient resources have been provided to support implementation.

While the emphasis on effectiveness and results is understandable, it is unfortunate, since a policy and/or program is just as likely not to succeed because of program failure as it is because of theory failure. Program failure can result from a number of different causes: the program contained a basic design flaw, insufficient instructions were communicated to critical actors essential to implementation, the effort encountered unexpected staff resistance, unanticipated events occurred, or circumstances didn't turn out as intended (Patton 1986).

Anyone who's ever tried to implement a policy and program has surely experienced many of these situations. Planners assumed health agencies would participate; and the agencies expressed a willingness to participate, but someone failed to realize there were legal restrictions that would take time to overcome before the health agencies could actually become involved. Or, no one knew the support staff would be opposed to their new roles in the new effort and would work skillfully and quickly to undermine it.

Obtaining a better understanding of implementation beforehand can minimize the likelihood of program failure and increase the possibility of policy being attained and service programs performing at an optimal level.

The Two Faces of Implementation

There are two sides to policy and program implementation. For Williams (1980), the two sides are "political feasibility" and "technical capacity." For Patton (1986), they are "technical feasibility" and "political viability."

The technical perspective on implementation treats functional concerns—the procedures and processes that need to be put in place. Success in the technical arena is dependent upon issues of capacity. Technical capacity involves the infrastructure, communication networks, resources, and operator skills possessed by the particular agency or system of agencies in which implementation is taking place (Williams 1975). Technical capacity concentrates on acquiring, strengthening, and sustaining the human and nonhuman capabilities and resources needed for implementation.

The political perspective acknowledges the importance of and attends to the numerous interpersonal, intergroup, and interorganizational issues that will inevitably arise in the course of implementation. By political we mean concerns that are an outgrowth of power relationships in the particular setting or settings where implementation is occurring. Success in the political sphere hinges on issues of feasibility. Political feasibility can be defined as "reconciling the diverse and occasionally conflicting interests of a range of many persons and groups with different stakes in the situation" (Vosburgh & Perlmutter 1984, p.110). Political feasibility focuses on the ability to deal with different sources of power in a particular environment in such a way as to either get their support and/or at least prevent them from subverting the implementation effort.

Even though it appears both political and technical factors should be attended to in any implementation situation, there is reason to believe it does not occur. While policy makers focus on political matters, it is not evident that they consistently deal with the feasibility of policy initiatives (Mazmanian & Sabatier 1981). Moreover, policy makers are likely to be even more removed from matters of technical capacity. In contrast, it often seems as if it is easier for program people to deal with and exert control over technical matters, especially as they relate to their own service agency. Addressing political affairs remains somewhat more elusive and far more difficult for program professionals to grapple with (Mannes 1990).

Strategies that can elicit both political and technical matters and promote the analysis of both are needed to expedite the implementation process and improve our understanding of it.

The Purpose of Conducting an Implementation Assessment

To foster policy and program implementation, it is essential to obtain a greater understanding of what may transpire as implementation proceeds. There is no way one can uncover all matters beforehand; but by employing a technique defined as "Implementation Assessment," many of the issues and factors that will eventually need to be addressed can be identified at the outset. By employing an Implementation Assessment, the possibility of program failure can be minimized.

Implementation Assessments need to be distinguished from Implementation Analyses. The former are used before implementation begins, while the latter are employed to evaluate an implementation effort after it has transpired.

Implementation Assessments serve as planning tools that can be quite useful to policy makers, administrators, and practitioners. They help identify a host of political and technical factors that need to be attended to if implementation is to proceed unimpeded and are especially useful when new policies and programs are being considered.

Implementation Assessments should adopt a "bottom-up" orientation, based upon the principle of "backward-mapping" as set forth by Elmore (1979-1980). This perspective argues that it is most important to assess implementation at the point of service delivery and to concentrate on the service delivery agencies and the staff of those organizations. Attention should be directed to where "street-level" bureaucrats and clients work, as opposed to the higher levels where policy makers and top administrators dwell (Elmore 1986; Williams 1975, 1982). Williams (1980), asserts the changes required by implementation can only be brought about by involving key agency units, and those individuals whose "status" and "jobs" may be affected, in the change process.

Implementation Assessments need to have a strong behavioral basis. Williams (1980) cites four areas about which an Implementation Assessment can offer insights and suggestions: 1) what direct service agency staff will do with nonhuman resources, 2) how staff from these agencies will work with each other, 3) how staff from these agencies might work with other vital parties, and 4) how they will treat those expected to benefit from their services.

Finally, Implementation Assessments must be able to uncover both technical and political concerns relevant to the implementation of a particular type of program in a particular setting.

CONDUCTING AN IMPLEMENTATION ASSESSMENT FOR FAMILY PRESERVATION SERVICES

An Implementation Assessment was conducted to identify issues related to the introduction of family preservation services in Indian Child Welfare settings in two distinct sites—the Upper Peninsula of Michigan and the Rio Grande Corridor of New Mexico. Planning teams were formed at each site, with team membership comprised primarily of direct service agency workers at the managerial and case practice levels from tribal government agencies, Indian nonprofit organizations, and state and non-Indian service agencies that were part of the community service network and needed to be involved in the implementation assessment process.

A technique known as Concept Mapping (Trochim 1989) was used in conducting the Implementation Assessment. Concept Mapping was used to gather and assess the perceptions of planning team members regarding implementation issues. According to Trochim (1989), planning typically involves conceptualization activity; and Concept Mapping helps groups organize and represent their thinking. The result of employing Concept Mapping is a picture or map of the major ideas generated by the group that shows how those ideas relate to each other. Concept Mapping insures that all participants have equal opportunities for input and allows a diverse group to focus its thinking.

The planning teams at both sites received a presentation on the structure and function of FPS. To complete the first step in Concept Mapping, each team was asked to brainstorm implementation issues in response to the following prompt:

> In order to get family preservation services operating:
>> What do you need to do?
>> What do you think needs to be done?
>> In other words, what needs to happen?
>> (Mannes 1989)

The brainstorming prompt used to generate the implementation issues is consistent with Williams' (1975) argument that implementation needs to focus concretely on getting a program operational. The prompt also was structured so respondents would not just consider what they needed to do but also would be motivated to think in a broader sense and consider what others might need to do to implement FPS.

The Michigan Team generated 91 issues, and the New Mexico Team developed a list of 53 issues. The author and an associate, Ying-Ying T. Yuan, reviewed both lists to identify redundancies and developed a master list which sought to accurately reflect the range of items produced by the members of both planning teams. The master list contained 81 implementation issues.

The second step in Concept Mapping involved asking all planning team members from both sites to sort the master list of issues into piles in a "way that makes sense to you." This was done to obtain a conceptual portrait of how the implementation issues were organized and interrelated in the minds of planning team members. This step also revealed how the implementation issues could be organized into clusters that represented broader implementation concerns.

Analysis and interpretation of the results of the sorting activity was accomplished by entering the data from the sorts into the Concept Mapping System software package developed by Trochim (1989). The data were subjected to several statistical procedures.

The first procedure used is known as multidimensional scaling (MDS). The result of the MDS analysis is a point map which can be found in Figure 1 on page 35. On the map, each of the 81 implementation issues is represented by a separate point. Issues which are perceived as being similar to each other—meaning they were placed in the same pile by many of the people who sorted—are close together on the map; less similar issues are farther apart on the map. To see this distinction, turn to Figure 1 and focus on the center-right portion of the map. One can conclude that issues 60 and 37 were sorted by more members of the planning teams into the same pile than issues 60 and 78. Hence, the points representing implementation issue 60 and 37 are closer together on the map than the points representing issues 60 and 78.

The next statistical procedure used was cluster analysis—essentially a classification technique. Ward's algorithm for hierarchical cluster analysis was employed to produce various groupings of points. The objective was to classify the 81 issues into clusters representing broader implementation concerns. Even though cluster analysis involves a degree of subjective discretion and judgment, it can be very suggestive in discerning categories within a particular set of items.

In cluster analysis procedures, it is customary to organize the set of items of interest into various numbers of clusters. In this application, the 81 implementation issues were organized into 25, 20, 15, 10, and six

34

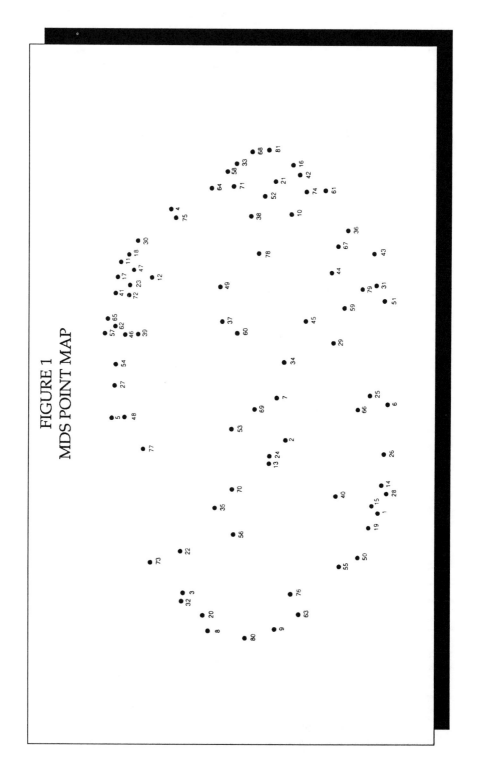

FIGURE 1
MDS POINT MAP

groups respectively. These various cluster solutions were then presented to each planning team. After review and discussion, it was agreed that the six-cluster solution served as the "best" means of making sense of the issues and defining important categories of implementation issues.

The author again reviewed the six-cluster solution for suitability; as a result, several additional changes and a number of deletions of issues were made. The final six-cluster solution map can be found in Figure 2 on page 37.

The next step in Concept Mapping was to have planning team members come up with names for the six clusters. A word count procedure—essentially a frequency-based content analysis (Krippendorff 1980)—was used to assess the naming activity. In the word count procedure, frequencies of word usage are tabulated, and those words with the highest rate of usage are considered the most appropriate descriptors for the various clusters. The following cluster names resulted from the analysis:

Cluster I	Community Education for Support
Cluster II	Coordination among Agencies
Cluster III	Family Identification for Services
Cluster IV	Funding
Cluster V	Program and Service Development
Cluster VI	Staff Training

The final set of 76 implementation issues organized by cluster can be found in Figure 3 on pages 38-39.

Clarifying the Results of the Implementation Assessment

A review of the implementation clusters and issues shows that both the technical and political sides of implementation discussed earlier are evident in the results of the Implementation Assessment (Mannes 1990).

Examination of the master list of implementation issues organized by cluster in Figure 3 reveals that some deal mostly with matters of political feasibility while others are concerned primarily with technical capacity. Whereas "organizing inter-tribal political efforts" (55) in Cluster I is mainly a political feasibility issue, "advertising, recruiting and hiring workers "(17) in Cluster VI is fundamentally a technical capacity issue.

While one could argue that there is a political and technical aspect to each implementation issue, one could also make the claim that most

FIGURE 2
FINAL SIX-CLUSTER SOLUTION MAP

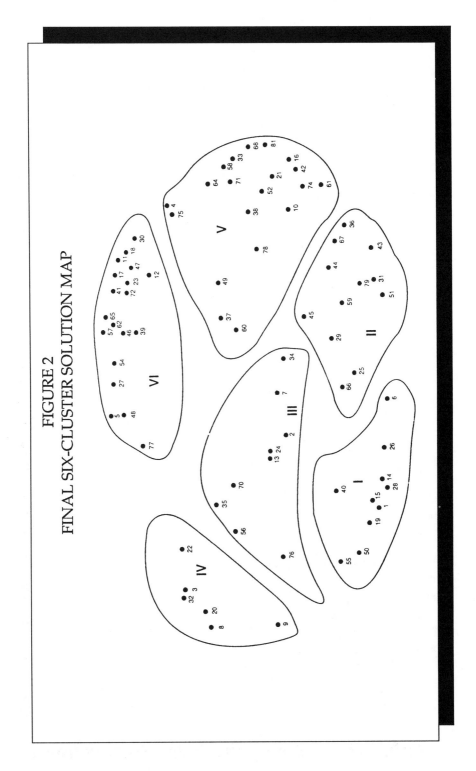

FIGURE 3
IMPLEMENTATION CLUSTERS AND
IMPLEMENTATION ISSUES
SPECIFIED BY PLANNING TEAM MEMBERS

Cluster I Community Education for Support
1 - educating the community to understand the need for family-based services
6 - getting community input into program design
14 - educating and gaining support of tribal council
15 - getting tribal council [governing body] to set family-based services as a top priority
19 - teaching the community about family-based services
26 - getting providers to inform community of availability or their interest in providing family-based services
28 - obtaining community support
40 - developing short position paper on Indian family-based services for tribes and Indian organizations
50 - conducting public relations efforts
55 - organizing inter-tribal political efforts

Cluster II Coordination among Agencies
25 - gaining support of other service providers
29 - obtaining data on number and type of current placements
31 - establishing inter-agency agreements
36 - coordinating for effective referrals
43 - examining the impact of changing services on existing agencies
44 - networking with courts
45 - establishing data base of families served
51 - cataloging existing resources
59 - reducing jealousies and turf issues
66 - establishing inter-agency coordinating council to identify, motivate, and foster collaborative relations
67 - coordinating with other providers to promote long-term goal of family unity
79 - strengthening existing programs before developing new [ones]

Cluster III Family Identification for Services
2 - defining who the family is
7 - assessing current caseload for service needs
13 - identifying families eligible for services
24 - distinguishing between chronic and "new" crisis families
34 - identifying the number and needs of dysfunctional families in the community
35 - providing concrete services, e.g., transportation
56 - working with families in a receptive environment
70 - focusing on the family unit
76 - training the non-Indian community to work effectively with Indian clients and agencies

Cluster IV Funding
3   -   identifying funding sources
8   -   having funding sources support tribal innovations
9   -   getting funding agencies to do less defending of turf
20 -   getting funding source(s) to provide child welfare dollars to support family-based services
22 -   securing funds (grantsmanship)
32 -   getting funds for training

Cluster V Program and Service Development
4   -   establishing qualifications for providing services
10 -   defining program from the tribal perspective
16 -   structuring services within Indian social services agencies
21 -   determining appropriate services for the program
33 -   setting program goals and objectives
37 -   being willing to terminate unsuccessful cases
38 -   distinguishing between prevention of abuse and neglect, and prevention of placement
42 -   defining service catchment area
49 -   setting realistic family goals
52 -   establishing a strong linkage to aftercare
58 -   developing service standards
60 -   retaining a flexible clinical approach
61 -   collecting information on other programs and adapting
64 -   generating program operations guidelines
68 -   developing research and evaluation plans
71 -   learning about culture and incorporating it into the program
74 -   identifying potential problems and barriers
75 -   choosing an appropriate approach, e.g., team or individuals
78 -   addressing creaming effects, i.e., "easier" cases are accepted, or "hardest" cases are referred
81 -   establishing service priorities

Cluster VI Staff Training
5   -   providing training on family-based services
11 -   considering staffing needs
12 -   reducing overlapping and/or conflicting roles of the workers
17 -   advertising, recruiting, and hiring workers
18 -   considering who and what type of workers are needed
23 -   establishing job descriptions
27 -   providing training in counseling
30 -   considering worker liability issues
39 -   training supervisors jointly with workers
41 -   recruiting committed and compassionate staff
46 -   providing a limited caseload for workers
47 -   having program manager who is a skilled social worker
48 -   providing ongoing education and training
54 -   upgrading workers' salaries
57 -   preventing high staff turnover
62 -   preventing worker burnout
65 -   providing worker incentive program
72 -   establishing appropriate supervision
77 -   having workers model appropriate behavior for families

issues have a dominant side, and they become either politically or technically dominant. For example, "getting funding source(s) to provide child welfare dollars to support family-based services" (20) in Cluster IV would seem to be an issue of political feasibility. Certainly there are technical means one could employ to educate funding sources and political leaders, above and beyond the more standard political lobbying and advocating efforts. Nevertheless, making issue (20) happen seems primarily dependent upon politics. In contrast, "developing service standards" (58) in Cluster V is a matter of technical capacity. There may well be political issues that need to be addressed in the defining of standards, but this issue risks characterization as primarily a technical exercise.

At the same time, there are some issues which are not clearly dominant one way or the other and are equally technical and political. "Securing funds (grantsmanship)" (22) in Cluster IV is an example of an issue that embodies roughly the same amount of technical expertise and political savvy.

The concepts of political feasibility and technical capacity are also evident in relation to the clusters identified and labeled by the planning teams. Each cluster can be defined as being either politically or technically dominant in the sense that a majority of the issues within it are either primarily political or technical in nature.

For example, Cluster I, Community Education for Support, seems to emphasize political feasibility. Most of the issues comprising it are political in that they involve building a base of support among relevant portions of the general public or working with the power structure and seeking the support of appropriate elected officials in order to implement FPS. In contrast, Cluster III, Family Identification for Services, seems to deal with matters of technical capacity. Issues like "assessing current caseloads for ascertaining service needs"(7) and "identifying the number and needs of dysfunctional families" in the community (34) involve technically determining who is eligible for the services so that appropriate organizational service delivery capabilities can be established.

This is not to say that a cluster is exclusively one way or the other. As was pointed out in the earlier discussion of implementation issues, there are technical facets to what are primarily political feasibility endeavors. Thus, for Cluster I, there are technical procedures that can be employed to foster community support. Likewise, even the most cut and dried technical concern can have political implications. The eligibility issues raised in Cluster III have a political dimension to them, as eligibility always does. Nevertheless, clusters of implementation issues, like individual issues, can be defined as having either a political or a technical emphasis.

In reviewing the implementation clusters, three seem to stress technical capacity and three seem to emphasize political feasibility. The three emphasizing technical capacity are:

Cluster III   Family Identification for Services
Cluster V   Program and Service Development
Cluster VI   Staff Training

The three stressing political feasibility are:

Cluster I   Community Education for Support
Cluster II   Coordination among Agencies
Cluster IV   Funding

MAKING USE OF THE IMPLEMENTATION ASSESSMENT RESULTS

The real utility of an Implementation Assessment goes beyond identifying the specific issues and broader categories of concern that must be dealt with in order to implement. It means using the information to make determinations about what actions need to be taken. An Implementation Assessment is a planning tool for facilitating implementation.

In the course of specifying the political and technical issues that must be addressed in establishing family preservation services in Indian Child Welfare settings, the overwhelming and perplexing sense of what has to be dealt with to get a program operational is organized in a meaningful and cogent manner and in a way that contributes to determining and planning appropriate responses.

Let's examine all six implementation clusters and consider what can be done to adequately respond to many of the issues contained in each. Remember that, even though each cluster is dealt with as if it were independent, in reality there are varying degrees of interdependence among all the clusters; and the work performed in one area has implications for the activity performed in others.

Cluster I
Community Education for Support

This cluster of implementation concerns focused on political support and endorsement efforts; a number of activities dealing with elected officials, the community, and other key groups were specified.

To garner political support, and in the process identify potential political opposition, the person(s) contemplating or responsible for implementation must seek answers to the following questions which are based on the work of Kaufman (1986).

- Who are the influential individuals and groups in the community that must be dealt with in establishing FPS?

- What are the influential individuals' and groups' beliefs and values regarding the introduction of the policy and program for FPS?

- How are decisions commonly made by each key group—by consensus, group bargaining, strong centralized leadership?

- What are the costs and the benefits (not just in terms of dollars and cents) to these specific individuals, power sources, and segments of the community, as well as to the general public, if FPS is adopted?

- Would any changes resulting from implementing FPS be temporary or permanent?

To answer these questions requires information in five crucial areas: 1) Basic Position; 2) Specific Concerns; 3) Likelihood of Involvement; 4) Resources; and 5) Relationships (Kaufman 1986).

Understanding Basic Position involves determining whether each influential group or individual is for, against, or neutral towards the program and whether each group will gain or lose directly or indirectly if FPS is implemented.

Specific Concerns deals with what each group or individual sees as especially important and potentially problematic. Some key aspects to examine here include: how controversial might FPS be, how much change is required to implement the program, how difficult the principles and justification for the program are to grasp, and whether it is seen as very complex to administer.

Elements such as salience, stake, and motivation are germane to determining Likelihood of Involvement. First, there is a need to clarify what each influential individual and/or group sees as being at stake for them with the introduction of family preservation services. Second, one must ascertain how motivated the individuals and/or groups are to actively

42

support or oppose the implementation effort.

The primary objective with Resources is to decide if groups and individuals have the time and money to become supporters or opponents of implementation. The category of Relationships is based upon whether groups and individuals have the power, legitimacy, knowledge, performance skills, and contacts to render support or organize opposition.

Once this information has been collected and analyzed and some degree of understanding has been attained, one can move on and initiate efforts to solidify political support or thwart opposition from groups and individuals.

According to Checkoway (1986), there are a number of activities one can pursue to obtain support. Several are described below.

- *Activating People*
  Mobilizing key community groups and individuals and securing their assistance can produce a lot of benefits. It creates avenues for obtaining important information program staff may have overlooked, improves overall information exchange, and provides a base from which to gain momentum required for implementation. In seeking support for FPS, staff should be willing to establish and maintain an honest dialogue with various groups of people and have a genuine interest in having them involved. The reasons why out-of-home placements are occurring, the impact dysfunctional families have on the community at large, and the ways in which the community can help in the effort should be addressed.

- *Educating People*
  The objective here should be to assist community members in learning about themselves and helping them understand a range of forces that influence them, their families, and their friends. Clarifying responses they can possibly make to alleviate problems that they and their loved ones are confronting is also crucial. Attention should be paid to what factors define the need for FPS in a community, how the program might impact individuals and their loved ones, and what suitable interventions can be created to deal with the difficulties. Determining appropriate channels for education, and using language that the community can understand, are vital. Far too often, unreasonable mediums are chosen and professional jargon makes the message incomprehensible. Personal outreach and public displays are options that seem suitable for educating the community about the need for family preservation services.

43

- *Establishing Relationships with Influentials*
  Indian communities are very small. Virtually everyone knows who the influential figures are in their settings. Some individuals and groups attain influence because of the position(s) they hold, while others are able to influence because of their reputations. Often, interest and support can be attained by resorting to influential persons' self-interest or by appealing to their known concern about an issue.

- *Actively Advocating for Family Preservation Services*
  Advocacy has always been centered around representing the interests and concerns of less powerful groups. Today there are many forms of advocacy, including legislative, administrative, legal, and electoral. Advocating for a program like FPS, and highlighting its merits before legislative, administrative, and other established entities within the community, is critical. These groups must be reminded of the urgency of the problems FPS will be addressing and clearly understand how the program will respond.

Developing a strategy to educate the community and key factions and then executing a plan to marshal their support is necessary when implementing family preservation services.

Cluster II
Coordination among Agencies

The second cluster consisted of implementation issues that also are mostly political in nature. Determining how to respond to interorganizational matters is essential, since an agency implementing FPS doesn't exist in a vacuum but in an environment comprised of a number of organizations. The agency implementing family preservation services will need to establish effective relations with organizations regarding referral processes, with agencies capable of providing therapeutic services, as well as with organizations capable of rendering aftercare services.

Establishing positive relations with other agencies requires some understanding of the ways in which organizations can relate. One critical dimension is the "tone" of the relationship being maintained between and among agencies. There are three tones: coordination, cooperation, and conflict (Hall 1982). Coordination involves organizations agreeing on a common goal and collaborating to accomplish it. For example, the school system, the court system, the mental health agency, and the social service organization all agree to make family preservation their common pursuit and work together to accomplish the goals of family preservation. Agencies can also have a tone of cooperation, meaning they orient their actions to a common outcome, but pursue their own goals and retain their autonomy. In this case, all the entities described above accept the importance of family preservation and try to honor the principle as they conduct their ongoing work. Both tones need to be distinguished from relationships marked by a tone of conflict, where one or more agencies will try to prevent another organization from implementing the program.

Interagency relations can also be distinguished by the "type" of relationship being maintained. There are four types of relationships: 1) ad hoc, 2) exchange, 3) formal agreement, and 4) the mandate (Hall 1982). Ad hoc relationships are transitory, typically one-shot in character, and preclude sustained contact. Hence, two agencies may work together to respond to the needs of one particular family; but there is no basis for ongoing associations. In the exchange relationship, both organizations recognize and honor a mutual need that the encounter fulfills. The exchange relationship results in benefits to all involved agencies. For example, the law enforcement agency works closely with the social service organization because both see the benefits of responding to the needs of juveniles under the rubric of family preservation ideals. The exchange relationship becomes formalized when the law enforcement authority and the social service agency providing FPS sign a Memorandum of Agreement to work together. Finally, in a mandate, either third parties or other powerful actors force agencies to work together regardless of whether they want to or not.

There are innumerable ways in which agencies can work together at the program level. Lauffer (1984) inventories a number of cooperative mechanisms available to agencies with regard to program implementation. Virtually all of the options are relevant to FPS:

case conferencing	program evaluation
case consultation	program operation
case management	purchase of services
co-location	referrals
needs assessments	facilities and equipment
intake, screening, and	staff
diagnosis	procedures
joint budgeting	technical assistance
loaner staff	staff development
program design	treatment teams

45

Often when attempting to obtain other agencies' support for implementing a new program like family preservation services, coalitions among agencies may have to be formed. One is most used to thinking of coalitions as political forces that come together and work together to achieve a common goal. In the context of implementation, coalitions can be broadly defined as entities that help agencies to coordinate their interests and interact in such a way as to advance their shared objectives. Agencies often band together to ward off a potentially disruptive political movement or to rally support for the passage of a particular policy and seek an appropriation to underwrite a certain program. Dluhy (1986) distinguishes among coalitions and identifies several varieties: informal, associations, and networks. The informal coalitions are single issue, loosely structured, and disappear once the specific objectives that sparked their formation have been accomplished. Associations or federations are more permanent, yet also have a limited scope. Networks are viewed as more permanent entities with the means to respond to a variety of issues and capable of continuously adapting to tackle new items as they emerge.

When organizing a coalition of any form, a number of factors must be taken into account: 1) how membership is defined and maintained, 2) what resources are available, 3) how functions and tasks are handled, and 4) how communication will be organized and managed (Dluhy 1986). For example: Will only agencies responding to the social needs of families and children be invited to participate, or will all human service agencies be asked to become a part of the family preservation coalition? Will a particular staff person in a particular agency be asked to plan and manage the affairs of the coalition, or will a task force of representatives from a number of agencies be asked to handle administrative tasks? Also, will there be a formal newsletter conveying important information, or will round-robin phone calling be the preferred method of staying in touch?

The competitive nature of the human service arena, where agencies are inclined to presume they secure and lose funds at the expense of other agencies, makes coordination among agencies vital to successfully implementing FPS. For FPS, a top agenda item becomes how to forge a coalition to link existing agencies and create an alliance to foster implementation.

Cluster III
Family Identification for Services

This cluster consisted of primarily technical implementation issues. The planning team members spotlighted concerns such as creating a response capacity for the target FPS population, along with closely related eligibility and assessment issues.

Eligibility is an important and complicated issue. Gates (1980) enumerates four standard criteria typically used in defining eligibility for social programs: 1) means-tested, 2) status, 3) compensatory, and 4) diagnostic.

In employing a means-tested criterion, one uses financial factors, such as clients' income or assets, as the basis for determining if they are eligible for the service. When using the status criterion, one considers clients' membership in an age group, a gender group, a community, etc., as the rationale for providing the service. The compensatory criterion responds to either those individuals or groups who have made important social and/or economic contributions (veterans), or who are at a great disadvantage in relation to the rest of society (the handicapped). Finally, the diagnostic criterion uses an assessment procedure to separate those clients who are eligible from those who are not.

For family preservation services, the criterion most likely employed would be diagnostic. But, as Gates (1980) points out, this approach to eligibility presents some problems. The biggest problem in using a diagnostic criterion to determine eligibility is that it is the least objective of the various criteria. For means-tested, status, and compensatory-based eligibility criteria, it has been possible to construct either theoretical or applied standards that are viewed as objective. Income levels and special status are clear and distinct. Diagnostic procedures, however, employed by doctors, psychiatrists, and social workers, depend greatly on individual discretion. Historically, programs that make use of diagnostic eligibility criteria have had to rely on professionalization and ethical codes as the basis for withstanding criticisms that they are operating in either an arbitrary or capricious fashion. Tribes or Indian nonprofits establishing FPS will need to thoughtfully and carefully develop standards for eligibility.

Adopting a particular FPS model has important implications for eligibility. (See the first article in this book for a description of the different types of FPS models.) The family-centered approach in FPS responds to families that have been self-referred or referred by another agency and are in need of assistance. The intensive family-centered crisis model responds exclusively to families with children who are at "imminent risk of placement." Diagnostic procedures to either screen referrals and determine who to serve or to gauge the risk of impending placement need to be instituted.

In a mixed FPS model containing aspects of 1) family education, support, and resource; 2) family-centered; and 3) family-centered intensive approaches, eligibility may be based on the nature of a family's presenting problems. For example, one group of families could be defined as those experiencing a "limited situational need." For this group of families, there may be a sudden event such as the unexpected loss of a job, or a family member may plunge the family into a temporary emotional or financial crisis. A second group of families could be defined as "multiproblem." These are families simultaneously experiencing a number of difficulties and caught up in what amounts to perpetual crisis.

Decisions about which families are eligible for the FPS program can be exceedingly difficult to make. Sometimes another set of even more painful decisions about which families will actually receive services must be made if resources available under FPS are insufficient to meet the total demand for the service. Making the hard determination about which families among those who are eligible will in fact be served can be especially trying. Available data, such as the distribution of problems among families in the community, that provides a rational basis for helping make the decision should be used.

This issue of diagnostics is also of major importance in the assessment of the needs of families. There is a growing trend in child protective services to use "decision-support instruments" to help case workers manage and interpret the data they are collecting on families. These tools and approaches provide information processing shortcuts and criteria by helping to organize data in a systematic manner, reduce the variation in the observation and description of data, establish rules for judgment to increase consistency and reliability of assessments, and determine what services to provide (Mannes, McDonald, & Yuan 1988).

The Child Well Being Scale developed for the Child Welfare League of America, The Risk Assessment Factor Sheet created by the State of Illinois, and the Family Function Rating Scale and Child Jeopardy Scale used by the Tulsa City-County Health Department are three of the many instruments currently in use. (The Yuan article in this volume discusses decision-support instruments in greater detail.)

Decision-support instruments often can improve the speed, accuracy, and consistency of judgments. While these instruments can assist the caseworker in certain decision-making areas, they do not replace the professional skills of caseworkers.

Making decisions about who will be served, focusing the intervention on the family unit, working with families in an appropriate setting, and using instruments to specify service needs are all essential issues involving the target population that must be resolved if the implementation of FPS is to occur in a smooth manner.

Cluster IV
Funding

The fourth category of implementation concerns identified by the planning teams involved finances. This cluster of issues clearly illustrates the point made earlier that there are certain clusters seen as equally encompassing matters of political feasibility and technical capacity.

There is a strong aspect of politics involved in implementation-related funding issues. Getting funding sources to appreciate the need for a certain service like FPS and engaging in advocacy and related processes to get the funding source to actually provide financial support are fundamental political tactics. Scanning the funding environment to see where grants and other forms of financial support may exist and making contact with those sources to ascertain how to organize and pitch your funding request also are often political in nature.

There is also the technical side of acquiring financial resources—an area that involves the mechanics and technical expertise to put together a proposal and respond to the specific requirements of a particular funding source.

Some general features of composing a proposal seeking financial support for FPS need to be mentioned. The discussion that follows is based on the work of Axelrod and Cooper (1986).

A proposal is a primary form of argumentative writing and requires the use of refined reasoning and problem analysis. At the most general level, a proposal for family preservation services should consist of an identified problem and a proposed solution.

The intent of the proposal is to persuade the funding source to accept the problem as legitimate, agree to the applicant's program response, and be willing to approve financial support for the project. To convince the funding source, the proposal writer discusses the problem in great detail, offering some background information on its causes that includes statistical data and perhaps detail on relevant historical events. In addition, the writer will outline how the proposed solution to the problem will be put in place. The proposal writer also needs to anticipate questions and concerns that the reviewer will have. Often, the writer must discuss the advantages and disadvantages of the proposed solution in comparison with potential alternative responses.

More details on how to accomplish these general proposal writing activities are presented below as steps.

Step I - Specify the problem
The proposal writer is obliged to:

- Define the problems facing families in the community and then clarify why the presence of dysfunctional families is a problem for the agency, the clients being served, and the community.

- Clarify the seriousness of the problem relative to other concerns the community faces, especially if family-based difficulties and the removal of children are seen as some of the biggest problems facing the community.

- Explain what are seen as the causes of the different problems facing families. Distinguish whether the problems are of a more recent origin or are long term.

- Describe the negative consequences of the problems. It also may be important to highlight different consequences for particular groups of families in the community.

- To review what's been written, return to the problems and reconsider whether they have been described in such a way that they can be seen by others as significant. Consider whether the funding source would develop concern about family-related problems in the community as a result of reading the proposal.

Step II - Identify a Tentative Solution
The key in this step is to employ creativity and be imaginative. In presenting responses to the problems, the writer will have the option of generating his or her own solution or applying the solutions that have been proposed by others to promote family preservation.

After thought, reading, and perhaps even conversations with others, articulate the most promising solution. Then generate all the tasks that will need to be undertaken to implement the solution.

Step III - Justify the Solution
The solution arrived at in Step II must seem practical and appropriate. It should also seem easy to implement. To strengthen the proposed solution and allow it to withstand the challenges and the questions of others, it should be reviewed in light of the following criteria:

- Its ability to solve the problem
- The cost of implementing it
- The time to implement it
- People's willingness to implement it
- How to initiate implementation
- Similar solutions that have been tried and found lacking
- Any apparent personal benefit it provides to the writer of the proposal

Answers to these questions should be retained because they play a key role when one gets to Step IV in this process.

Another way of making sure the proposed solution is sufficiently justified is to brainstorm all the reasons for making use of the proposed solution. Then, review the list to see which appear the most powerful and persuasive, and make sure those reasons have been included in the proposal narrative. Sometimes it may even be useful to brainstorm alternative solutions, then work through them laying out the advantages and disadvantages of each. The writer is then in a position to adapt the proposed solution and incorporate some advantages associated with other solutions.

Step IV - Review What You've Written with an Eye on the Reader
In any writing assignment, the goal is to write for a particular audience. With a proposal, the audience members serve as the reviewers of the proposal. Consequently, the writer always needs to consider who the reviewers are likely to be. A number of key questions need to be thought about:

- How knowledgeable are the reviewers likely to be about the topic of family preservation? How knowledgeable are the reviewers likely to be about Indian Child Welfare?
  For example, if they are quite knowledgeable about the Indian Child Welfare Act (ICWA) and Indian environments, a certain level of dis-

51

cussion on background and context setting can be avoided. If they are not, this kind of information will probably need to be included.

- Why might family-related problems be important to the reviewers and why would they feel the need to have the problems solved?

- Might the reviewers be allied with a particular viewpoint or perspective that would influence the degree to which they are willing to sanction what you're proposing?
  If the proposal is going to be reviewed by people from the mental health field, they will probably be supportive of psychotherapeutic interventions.

Bear in mind that these are only the most general guidelines to use in the formulations of a proposal for FPS. It is always essential that one review the content of the proposal against the established evaluation criteria.

Funding is, of course, essential. Without it there can be no family preservation services. Researching and developing proposals for funding creates the possibility for implementation to occur.

Cluster V
Program and Service Development

A number of implementation issues were consolidated by planning team members in the general area of designing the program and its services. Many of the implementation issues cited by planning team members within the Program and Service Development cluster were by and large technical in nature. Most issues dealt with common developmental tasks like setting goals, establishing procedures and practices, etc. The issues also involved organizing and integrating the structure of the program with the delivery of services.

An agency wishing to implement FPS should establish specifications for quality case management and come up with policies and procedures at all of the major case management milestones to guide case practice and service delivery. These major milestones would include: 1) establishing and directing a well-organized system for referrals, 2) registering families for services, 3) opening cases and conducting some type of family assessment, 4) developing service plans for the families, 5) providing services, 6) monitoring progress of the family with regard to the provision of services, 7) reviewing cases to gauge progress, and 8)

52

closing or rendering cases inactive. Decisions must be made about what will be done at all of these milestones so that the necessary apparatus, processes, standards, rules, and data collection mechanisms are spelled out and the smooth delivery of FPS can result.

A number of the implementation issues in this cluster focused on the topic of determining objectives and establishing intervention strategies. Goals and objectives are often confused. According to Patti (1983), goals are "statements that express a program's long-range intent to eliminate, reduce, or ameliorate a problem or need in the community. They reflect values and conditions to which we aspire, and thus provide a sense of purpose and direction, but they are seldom specified at a level of concreteness or within a time frame that permits evaluation" (p. 78).

Raia (1974) sees objectives as operationalized statements of program intent that express in specific, observable, and preferably measurable terms those changes (outcomes) the program seeks to produce within some designated time period.

The creation of sound objectives is difficult. The following suggestions are offered to formulate quality objectives:

- They start with the word "to" followed by an action verb.
- They specify a single key result to be accomplished.
- They specify a target date for accomplishment.
- They are as specific and quantitative as possible.
- They specify "what" and "when" and not "why" and "how".
- They are realistic and attainable.
- They are consistent with the resources available or anticipated.
- They are congruent with agency planning and policies.
  (Dobrec, Lester, & Mannes 1989)

Some examples of appropriate objectives would be:

- To provide intensive family-centered services to ten (10) families (where the child(ren) are at imminent risk of placement) during the first year of the FPS program, and prevent having to place the child(ren) from eight (8) families in substitute care for a period of at least one year following the introduction of services.

- To deliver family-centered casework services to fifteen (15) families (who are in need) during the first year and a half of the FPS program, and as a result prevent the presenting problem requiring social service intervention from reoccurring in ten (10) families for at least a nine-month period following the provision of services.

While program objectives explain what will be changed as a result of implementing FPS, they do not reveal how the changes will occur. This aspect is clarified by deciding what intervention strategies will be employed in the program. There are a number of frameworks for clarifying among service strategies. The one set forth by Schoenberger & Williamson (1977) is a useful illustration; it distinguishes among seven different strategies:

1. Education
2. Prevention
3. Treatment
4. Rehabilitation
5. Regulation
6. Supporting or strengthening existing programs
7. Generating institutional change

Treatment is a major intervention strategy for FPS. In making decisions about treatment, a number of factors need to be examined. For one, what will be the primary treatment approach? Will it be behaviorally based and include the development of social skills, or will it stress structural family therapy? For another, what will be the primary treatment goals? Will they be to strengthen the caretaker abilities of parents, or to have parents learn about anger management, overcome chemical dependency, or develop communication skills?

Each community exploring the possibilities of implementing FPS, or having made the decisions and determining how to proceed, will need to assess its needs and resources and determine the right treatment approach.

Even though politically oriented implementation issues for this cluster were not specified by the planning teams, several common and potentially problematic issues need to be briefly mentioned.

Any new program winds up placing new demands on the agency's administrative structure. The potential consequences of implementing a new program need to be examined early on in order to minimize any sudden and disruptive impacts of implementation.

One must be especially attentive to how the new program will be integrated or coordinated with other existing programs being managed by the parent agency. Of central importance is how smoothly the new effort can be absorbed into ongoing operations, minimizing disruptiveness. It is easy for a new effort to be perceived as competing for clients, funds, and other resources. In many instances, a new initiative—

54

especially one like FPS—might not be very clearly understood by agency personnel and even seen as running counter to already set agency goals. Meetings and discussions among all agency staff need to be conducted so that there is a clear understanding of the role of the new FPS project and how it can and will be integrated with existing efforts.

Responding to the implementation issues contained in this cluster produces the guiding framework that clarifies how clients move through each component of the program and each stage of services. The result is an overall blueprint for how the program will perform and discharge its duties. Developing the family preservation services program and designing its services remains a basic implementation task that must be tackled with rigor and sensitivity.

Cluster VI
Staff Training

In the sixth cluster, also, the planning teams tended to emphasize issues related to technical capacity. The planning team members were well aware that the introduction of a new program like FPS necessitates the training of existing staff or the hiring of new personnel to perform program tasks. There is no need to discuss this topic at length, since the article by Ronnau et al. in this publication goes into detail on the kinds of values, skills, and abilities needed by workers providing family preservation services.

Several general thoughts, however, are worth mentioning. The decision to implement FPS forces the agency to consider some broad personnel issues. If existing staff are to be retrained, sensitivity to and understanding of their long-standing roles, behaviors, and orientations are important. If the agency needs to look elsewhere for staff, it must establish and carry through on quality recruitment and selection procedures. Agency management must be prepared to create job descriptions that are realistic and task based and make sure there are procedures in place to conduct performance evaluations. Ongoing staff development plans also must be drawn up. Managers responsible for the implementation of FPS must recognize the fundamental connections between quality personnel management and implementation, and the direct relation these two elements have to program effectiveness.

CONCLUSION

The set of implementation issues and more general implementation concerns related to the planned introduction of a family preservation services program in Indian Child Welfare settings that were generated by two planning teams in the course of conducting an Implementation Assessment are extremely valuable. The six implementation clusters and the 76 implementation issues resulting from the Implementation Assessment are by no means presented as an exhaustive and comprehensive account of what must be dealt with to implement a family preservation program in an Indian setting. Nevertheless, by identifying a wide range of factors that should be attended to, the clusters and issues serve as a useful inventory of implementation concerns. Suggestions on how to respond to all of the general categories of implementation concerns and many of the most important implementation issues within each cluster can expedite the introduction of FPS.

Implementing family preservation services will be a challenge—a challenge that many Indian communities may decide they have no choice but to face. Hopefully, the ideas and activities described in this article will turn the challenge into a learning situation and result in a positive experience for all those involved in the implementation process.

REFERENCES

Axelrod, R.B., & Cooper, C.R. (1986). *The St. Martin's guide to writing.* New York: St. Martin's Press.

Bardach, E. (1977). *The implementation game: What happens after a bill becomes a law.* Massachusetts: The MIT Press.

Checkoway, B. (1986). Political strategy for social planning. In B. Checkoway (Ed.), *Strategic perspectives on planning practice.* Massachusetts: Lexington Books.

Dobrec, T., Lester, S., & Mannes, M. (1989). *Grantsmanship manual.* Oklahoma/New Mexico: Three Feathers Associates, American Indian Law Center, Inc.

Dluhy, M.J. (1986). Developing coalitions in the face of power: Lessons from the Human Services. In B. Checkoway (Ed.), *Strategic perspectives on planning practice.* Massachusetts: Lexington Books.

Dye, T.R. (1972). *Understanding public policy.* New Jersey: Prentice-Hall, Inc.

Elmore, R.F. (1979-80). Backward mapping: Implementation research and policy decisions. *Policy Science Quarterly,* 94, winter, 601-616.

Gates, B.L. (1980). *Social program administration: The implementation of social policy.* New Jersey: Prentice-Hall, Inc.

Hall, R. H. (1982). *Organizations: Structure and process.* New Jersey: Prentice-Hall, Inc.

Kaufman, J.L. (1986). Making planners more effective strategists. In B. Checkoway (Ed.), *Strategic perspectives on planning practice.* Massachusetts: Lexington Books.

Krippendorff, K. (1984). *Content analysis: An introduction to its methodology.* California: Sage Publications.

Lauffer, A. (1984). *Strategic marketing for not-for-profit organizations: Program and resource development.* New York: The Free Press.

Mannes, M., McDonald, W., & Yuan, Y.T. (1988). *Strengthening decision-making. A handbook for Indian Child Welfare program staff.* New Mexico: American Indian Law Center, Inc.

Mannes, M. (1989). Using concept mapping for planning the implementation of a social technology. *Evaluation and Program Planning,* 12, 67-74.

Mannes, M. (1990). The perceptions of human service workers in planning for the implementation of the family preservation services innovation in Indian child welfare settings. Unpublished Dissertation. New York: Cornell University.

Mazmanian, D.A., & Sabatier, P.A. (1981). *Effective policy implementation.* Massachusetts: Lexington Books.

McGowan, B. (1988). Family-based services and public policy: Context and implications. In J.K. Whittaker, J. Kinney, E.M. Tracy, & C. Booth (Eds.), *Improving practice technologies for workers with high risk families:*

Lessons from the homebuilders social work education project. Washington: Center for Social Work Research, University of Washington.

Patti, R.J. (1983). *Social welfare administration: Managing social programs in a developmental context.* New Jersey: Prentice-Hall, Inc.

Patton, C.V. (1986). Policy analysis with implementation in mind. In B. Checkoway (Ed.), *Strategic perspectives on planning practice.* Massachusetts: Lexington Books.

Raia, A.P. (1974). *Managing by objectives.* Illinois: Scott Foresman.

Schoenberger, E., & Williamson, J. (1977). *Deciding on priorities and specific programs.* Washington, D.C.: International City Managers Association.

Trochim, W.M.K. (1989). An introduction to concept mapping for planning and evaluation. *Evaluation and Program Planning, 12,* 1-16.

Vosburgh, W.W., & Perlmutter, F.D. (1984). The demonstration project: Politics amidst professionalism. In F.D. Perlmutter (Ed.), *Human services at risk.* Massachusetts: Lexington Books.

Weiss, C. H. (1972). *Evaluation research.* New Jersey: Prentice-Hall, Inc.

Williams, W. (1975). Implementation analysis and assessment. *Policy Analysis, 2,* 531-566.

Williams, W. (1980). *The implementation perspective: A guide for managing social service delivery programs.* California: University of California Press.

Williams, W. (1982). The study of implementation: An overview. In W. Williams (Ed.), *Studying implementation: Methodological and administrative issues.* New Jersey: Chatham House Publishers, Inc.

Home-Based Family Therapy: A Model for Native American Communities *

NADINE TAFOYA

INTRODUCTION

Home-Based Family Therapy (HBFT) with Native American families is a treatment modality that can provide optimal therapeutic benefits to both the individual and the family. HBFT is an approach that utilizes an integral part of Native American culture itself—the bond of the family, the extended family, and the community. HBFT draws upon the natural strength and value of this phenomenon to emphasize the positive qualities buried within intergenerational dysfunctional behavior.

A MODEL FOR HOME-BASED FAMILY THERAPY

Within the past decade there has been a growing desire for mental health professionals to develop programs that will meet the needs of culturally diverse populations. Social problems in Native American communities, such as alcoholism, drug abuse, suicide, and teen pregnancies, to name a few, are topics that have all been addressed with urgent fervor. These topics have been the subjects of articles, research studies, and discussions at almost every conference where Indian issues are being addressed. For some Native American communities, their efforts to develop culturally sensitive program models have proven a partial success. The purpose of this article is to discuss an intervention model that may be the key to the successful interruption in those social problems which have spiraled Indian communities toward the lowest socioeconomic class in this country.

Current studies in the fields of addictions and family violence have shown linkages between these problems and the interrelationships of

* Many people were instrumental in making this program a success. This author would like to thank those Native American families that risked fear and uncertainty and yet stayed with the program. In addition, a special heart-felt thanks to my good friend, Nanci Mon. Without her help this article could not have been completed.

family members (Black 1987; Bradshaw 1989). It is a shared belief among many clinicians that for individuals suffering from certain types of behavioral disorders such as, addictions, physical violence, depression, and suicidal tendencies, an effective treatment method is to work with the entire family system (Steinglass et al. 1987).

Other research indicates that the roots of these problems in American Indian society is imbedded in a historical legacy of loss of land, genocide, racism, and forced assimilation (Middleton-Moz 1986; Jordan 1987, 1989; Tafoya 1989).

Family-Centered Intervention Services is a concept that is proving itself as a viable method of prevention/intervention for American Indian families. Home-Based Family Therapy is a crucial component of this concept. This is partially due to the fact that, historically, the family has always been the strongest link within the Indian community.

Family-based intervention emphasizes the family rather than the individual child or adult as a focus of the service. Working within this context, one is able to address multiple problem areas including addictions, violence, resistance to treatment, conflicting values and goals, and identity confusion. It can even include addressing basic social service needs (Mannes & Yuan 1988).

The intention of most well-planned family intervention/prevention programs is to assure that the family unit is preserved and that individuals within the family unit are functioning at their maximum potentials. Thus, every effort is made by the clinical practitioner to identify symptomatic behavior, to understand the underlying causes of the behavior, and then to examine the mechanisms being utilized to manage such behavior. The clinician then poses certain strategies to the family that will impact the system. Opportunities are provided for the family to try out new behaviors, and the clinician supports active changes that will lessen the dysfunctional behaviors and, eventually, lead to the restructuring of the entire family system (Steinglass et al. 1987).

Theoretical Framework for Home-Based Family Therapy

The theoretical framework for the Home-Based Family Therapy program is taken primarily from two different models of family therapy—the Structural and the Strategic Family Therapy models and techniques developed by Haley, Minuchin, and Montalvo, who are pioneers in this field. Although there are differences between these two approaches, they share certain commonalities. Stanton (1981) summarizes these similarities as:

60

- People are seen as interacting within a context—both affecting it and being affected by it.

- The family life cycle and developmental stage are important both in diagnosis and in defining therapy strategy.

- Symptoms are both system-maintained and system maintaining.

- The family can change, allowing new behaviors to emerge, if the overall context is changed. Further, in order for individual change to occur, the interpersonal system itself must change. This would permit different aspects of family members (potential) "character" to emerge.

In addition to working within a therapeutic framework, the HBFT therapist must be aware of some cultural nuances that will impact the therapy session. This was alluded to earlier when it was stated that family therapy is a viable approach when working with American Indian families because of the strong ties among family members.

The word "family" refers to not only a primary nuclear unit of individuals (mother, father, children) but to a large group of extended family members (grandparents, aunts, uncles, and cousins). There are those people who are also counted as "family" who are not blood-related. These include in-laws, godparents, clan members, marital sponsors, and others related by traditional religious alliances (Attneave 1981).

This author asked a group of Native American social workers to describe a "typical" family from their community. They were also asked to reflect on some of the problems the American Indian family is facing today. Some of their responses follow:

They all agree that women are perceived as the strong ones in the family. This observation is made though women seldom have the recognition or the power inherent to such a role. The woman, as a wife, mother, or grandmother, provides the foundation for family life.

A negative twist to the perception of the strong Native American woman develops when the wife and mother becomes "super mom." As her co-dependent tendencies take over, she becomes super responsible and controlling. With the ever-increasing responsibilities on her shoulders, she develops a martyr stance: "I'm expected to take care of everything!" or "They all depend so much on me." This type of role, especially in a two-parent family, can create negative attitudes among family members. Mother assumes responsibility for the overall caretaking of the family, including caring for her husband as if he were one of the children, and father steps down as the head of the household. This diminishes any support given by the husband and dissolves the partnership of the two parents. The children, then, may develop negative perceptions of adult male figures in the family. It is at this point that many families begin to experience family chaos. Mother becomes exhausted and resentful of her family because she's carrying all the burdens, father tries to escape his feelings of worthlessness through some type of addiction, and the children are out of control—defying parental authority, using drugs or alcohol, and/or experiencing feelings of fear and confusion.

The role of men, the social workers say, as the respected traditional leaders and sole wage earners of the family is disappearing. The decline of these strong male role models in the family and in the community has had a tremendous impact on the tribe as a whole. That is, when a man is no longer the recognized head of the family and does not hold a position that is meaningful to the community, he has lost a significant place in his culture—a place that traditionally defined his whole identity. The clinician recognizes that these problems can manifest as alcoholism or other addictions (sex, work, food, rage), physical or somatic illness, depression, and suicide.

Another value that the group mentioned as disappearing is the concept of community and cooperation. Historically, individuals within the community were the concern of the entire village. "Today, we experience indifference," they said. "People are hesitant to get involved in their neighbor's problems." Yet, some of the social workers stated that they remembered when children of the village were cared for collectively and that everyone had the responsibility for teaching children the traditional ways. Unfortunately, these social workers sometimes found it difficult to make foster care placements for children, even among their own extended family members.

The social workers felt that the Indian community is going through a time of incredible transitions. Although some of these changes have been positive, they felt that many of the values and cultural traditions have been negatively impacted.

The social workers said that the grandmothers and grandfathers can't understand the "children of the sixties.... They think it was a time when we began to experience a rapid deterioration of the traditional lifestyle and loss of our culture," they said. "The old ones think that this generation of adults will be the last to speak the language, and practice the cultural ways, such as ceremonial rituals, songs and dances. They see the communal lifestyle already disappearing with the building of government housing. We no longer live in close proximity to our relatives. We aren't concerned about our families' problems, anymore," was their despairing remark.

Although most of the social workers thought that family ties are still very much intact, family "support" can be dysfunctional. Mirroring the general population, denial of existing problems runs high: "As long as it's not bothering me... ." Enabling behaviors are the norm: "poor thing, his friends always make him do it... ." The treatment process is misunderstood and unrealistic: "Can you fix her?"

Fortunately, the social workers are not discouraged by the seemingly overwhelming amount of work that needs to be done in Indian communities. Rather, they are heartened by knowing what lies within their midst; and they focus their efforts on the threads of inherent strengths that weave through the fabric of Indian values, culture, and traditions— all of which, they believe, are at the heart of the Native American person.

The Behavior and Strategy of the Home-Based Therapist

In their paper, "Home-Based Therapy with American Indian Families," Schact, Tafoya, and Mirabel (1989) describe components that proved necessary for more effective therapeutic outcomes. They state that "some common features of healing include aspects of the relationship between the client and the helper [which] includes sensitivity to designated locales, as places of healing, rationales or myths to explain the problem, and tasks or procedures prescribed by the rationale to effect healing" (p.7).

Before moving into the next section detailing two case studies, it is important not only to attend to the daily struggles of these families, but also to be observant of the therapist's role as the change agent. The therapist is, while conversing with the family in a benign way, also plotting strategies for changes in the behavior and responses of the family.

At the onset, the therapist is paying particular attention to certain details. These include:

- Notice the structuring of the inside of the house. Is the environment conducive to family interaction?

- What is the overall atmosphere of the home? Did the presence of strangers effect the atmosphere? Could one sense if the feelings were relaxed, tense, or guarded?

- How does the family gather? What does one observe about space between members and/or physical touching?

- Observe the interaction among family members. Are there any verbal or non-verbal exchanges? Are there any responses regarding intimacy, verbal or nonverbal?

- Make observations regarding "family rules." How can these be defined? Who provides directives, of any kind, toward each other or toward the therapist? Who assumes the lead? Observe the eye contact between family members. Do they look at each other and the therapist? In what way?

- Pay attention to the conversation that takes place between family members or with the therapist. What is the affect and level of animation among family members? Is it spontaneous or flat? What is observed regarding the sense of relationship among family members? What are the relationship boundaries among the family and extended family? Are they appropriate, enmeshed, or distant?

- Is the family able to organize itself in appropriate fashion to address a task?

Criticisms and Barriers to Implementing HBFT in Indian Communities

Past experience with the Western medical model of "treatment" hasn't been very effective for the most part and it hasn't addressed the historical pain. Although Family-Based Therapy is a Western-style approach to therapy, this model has been adapted to utilize the strengths and cultural norms of the traditional Indian family system, making it one of the most successful models used in such settings to date.

Many Western approaches separate the individual from the family and community. Therapy takes place in an impersonal office setting. HBFT takes place in the family home, though some practitioners might feel uncomfortable providing therapy in a setting other than an office.

Confidentiality is one of the major issues threatening the progress of HBFT programs. One of the main criticisms of HBFT programs concerns the leaking of private information out into the community. Sometimes the families themselves will reveal their problems to other relatives or friends, and it is at this point that the gossip begins to circulate within the community. There must be a detailed and sensitive procedure for notifying families of their referral to HBFT services. In most cases, the referral comes from tribal court or social services; and self referrals also can be made.

The non-Indian therapist, it should be noted, will be perceived as a "stressor" to the family, creating another problem to overcome. However, this is not a major issue and can be turned into a positive asset. In some instances the fact that the therapist is non-Indian, unfamiliar with community gossip, and not related to community members, can negate some of the hesitancies a family might have about working with a person from outside of their own culture. However, once either the Indian or non-Indian therapists become known, their visits to families do not go unnoticed by the rest of the community. This is especially true in cases where there has been public fervor surrounding either the individual or the situation.

Essential components of a successful HBFT program are flexibility, few time constraints, support, and supervision. Unfortunately, most community mental health programs answer to a bureaucracy that enforces restrictive policies relating to management of time and resources. Because of heavy client loads, supervision becomes a luxury that few agencies can afford, and paper work becomes a priority. This author recognizes the shortcomings of community mental health programs; however, this should not rule out experimentation with the model.

HOME-BASED FAMILY THERAPY:
A WORKING MODEL

The description that follows is of a community-based Family Therapy Program that was a component of a Family Services Program. The Family Therapy Program was developed by the director of a Southwest Indian Health Service Hospital (P.H.S.-I.H.S.) Mental Health program. The hospital served 12 Indian reservations, plus a large number of Indian people who lived in the nearby off-reservation community. Within the Service Unit area were four community-based health centers. The major populations served were 11 Pueblo tribes and one Apache tribe. However, as indicated earlier, the hospital also serviced a variety of Indian families who were members of tribes from throughout the country.

Three mental health therapists were contracted by IHS to provide services within the Family Services Program to these communities. Two of the therapists were MSW's, while the third was an MA level psychologist. All three had specialized training in Strategic/Structural Family Therapy, as well as training and experience in the fields of alcoholism, drug addictions, domestic violence, and child abuse and neglect.

Two of the therapists were non-Indian, and the third was Native American but a member of a tribe from a different area. These differences posed some interesting problems, with both positive and negative results. None of the three therapists had been raised in any of the communities in which they were working; however, the Indian therapist was married and living in one of the communities in the Service Unit area. All three therapists had worked three years or more among the various Indian communities prior to being contracted by IHS and were familiar with the social structures, norms and values, and community resources available. Again, having this familiarity proved to be a valuable asset to the team.

Protocol for the Initial Visit to the Family

The protocol for the initial visit from the therapist was to have a Notice of Referral sent to the family by the Family Service Program. The notice stated who had referred the family, the reason for the referral, and the time and date of the expected visit to the home by the therapist.

The following case studies illustrate the practical application of HBFT in an Indian community. The case studies are composites of numerous families seen throughout a five-year period. The names used are all fictitious. Genograms depicting the family relationships for each case study are included.

Case Study No. 1: Rios Family

Fermin Rios was a divorced thirty-nine year old father of two. He had custody of his children, Danny, age 11, and Rita, age 14. The family lived with Fermin's elderly parents since he was the only child of Charley and Rebecca Rios, ages 81 and 75, respectively.

The therapist became involved with the Rios family when the tribal court referred Fermin to the Family Services Program for repeated public drunkenness and for allegedly assaulting his elderly parents on several occasions.

The family lived in a traditional adobe house that Fermin's grandfather had built. When Fermin married, Charley added on several extra

FIGURE 1
GENOGRAM OF THE RIOS FAMILY

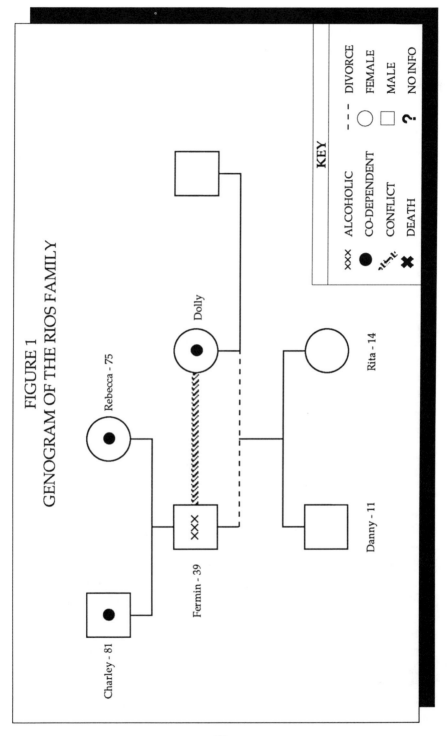

rooms so that all could co-exist comfortably.

Charley Rios was a farmer. Despite his advancing years, he annually cultivated a 12-acre plot with sweet corn, hay, alfalfa, and beans. In addition, both he and Rebecca tended a small garden located behind their house. Here they raised several varieties of colored corn for ceremonial purposes, chile, and a few vegetables.

On the first visit to the home, the therapist was greeted by the elderly parents. Fermin Rios was nowhere in sight. When asked if Fermin was home, Charley and Rebecca only gestured, "He's around." The therapist did not react negatively to this information and quickly dismissed the topic.

The hour was spent discussing family backgrounds. The therapist, being Native American, disclosed her tribal heritage, her marital status, and her experience working with members of the community. The elderly couple talked of their family history, the family's accomplishments, and how they now spend their time. Rebecca served a light refreshment of ice water and Indian cookies.

Although Fermin and his children were fluent in both their native language and English, Charley and Rebecca barely understood English and conversed primarily in their native language. The therapist, who did not speak the native tongue, communicated with Charley and Rebecca using simple words and phrases, hand gestures, and metaphors. Example:

"Why does Tano (Fermin) get that way? Doesn't he know it's no good?" Charley asks the therapist, referring to Fermin's alcoholism.

The therapist responds, "When Tano starts his drinking, he can't stop. Think as if Tano were going hunting in the desert. And that he was going to be in the desert for three days. He takes with him only three canteens of water to last him for those three days. Once Tano begins to sip on the first canteen of water, he would not be able to stop drinking the water. It would be as if his throat were so dry he couldn't get enough to drink. He would continue to drink the water until all the canteens were empty. Tano would know that he needs to save his water, but he wouldn't be able to stop drinking it. That's what it's like when you have the disease of alcoholism."

At this stage, the therapist was building trust and being assessed by the family. They were deciding if this was a person they could relate to, and if this person would understand them care about them and guide them to some understanding of their pain. A family will not be impressed by the therapist's educational background, the degree(s) they hold, or by titles or letters (MSW, Ph.D.) on their calling cards. Instead, the therapist is judged on his/her sensitivity to traditional protocols, including being respectful to the elders, informing them of their family history, what their relationship is to the community, and by displaying patience.

Eventually, Fermin showed up and was introduced to the therapist. Rebecca stood, indicating informally that she and Charley would depart, leaving the two of them alone in the room. Before leaving, she nodded to Fermin with a look that seemed to say,"It's okay, go ahead and talk." With that, she turned away closing the door behind her. During the next hour the problems of alcohol abuse and Fermin's episodic assaults on his family were discussed. A therapeutic relationship had been established, and therapy was beginning.

The interview that took place gave the therapist the following information:

- Fermin was currently unemployed, and hadn't been able to hold on to a steady job due to his drinking.

- The Rios family had no car nor any viable means of transportation.

- Fermin had been court ordered into the community alcoholism treatment center five times in the last two years.

- Fermin had been divorced for two years from his wife of ten years and that his former wife, Dolly, had just remarried six months ago. She was now living in another community.

- Fermin's children were average students in school with no apparent behavior problems.

- The family was living on Charley's and Rebecca's social security income, as well as receiving some food stamps and food staples from the commodity food program.

In considering the above information about the family, the therapist decided to pursue the issue of Fermin's isolation from his family, the land, and his community, due to his problem drinking.

The therapist: "Fermin, there is always so much activity going on here in the village. Was it always this way? Can you remember what kinds of things you were involved in as a young man?"

Fermin: "It's busy around here because everyone's getting ready for

69

planting season. There's a lot that needs to be done before we actually start planting. First, we need to get the irrigation ditches cleaned out, then the fields have to be tilled. When I was younger, there was a Spanish man that used to come around with his tractor and plow. He would plow everyone's fields because all we had was horse-drawn plows. My cousin and I would follow him from field to field because whenever he was ready to take a break, he would let us drive the tractor."

As Fermin related the tales of his younger days, it was apparent that he had once been very involved in the traditions of the village. And because the community was agrarian, there were many functions that followed the planting and harvesting of crops, including ceremonial rituals and social events. However, because of his problem drinking, he was ashamed and no longer participated in the activities of the community.

The therapist used this avenue to further engage Fermin in therapy and to establish a direction out of Fermin's downward spiral of addiction. After the initial home visit with Fermin and his family, the therapist made arrangements to meet with the family on a weekly basis. In the beginning, the therapist met with Fermin individually. They discussed his alcoholism and its impact on his life. Eventually, the weekly therapy session included the whole family. The focus of the therapy was alcohol education, opening up communication among family members, talking about feelings, and practicing new behaviors that would counteract negative enabling behaviors.

Therapy lasted six months. Upon termination, the clinical assessment was that all family members had gained some insight into their problem areas. They practiced new coping mechanisms which eventually led to permanent changes in the dynamics of their interpersonal family relationships.

Case Study No. 2: The Blacktail Family

In families where the children are being physically abused, indications are that the parents were usually victims of abuse in their own families of origin.

This was the case in the Blacktail family. Tim was 27 years old. He and his twin brother, Ralph, had been abandoned by their alcoholic parents when they were two months old. They were raised in the Pueblo of their maternal grandparents.

Grandfather Blacktail died when Tim was 15 years old. He had been a chronic alcoholic and was very cruel to both of the boys. When

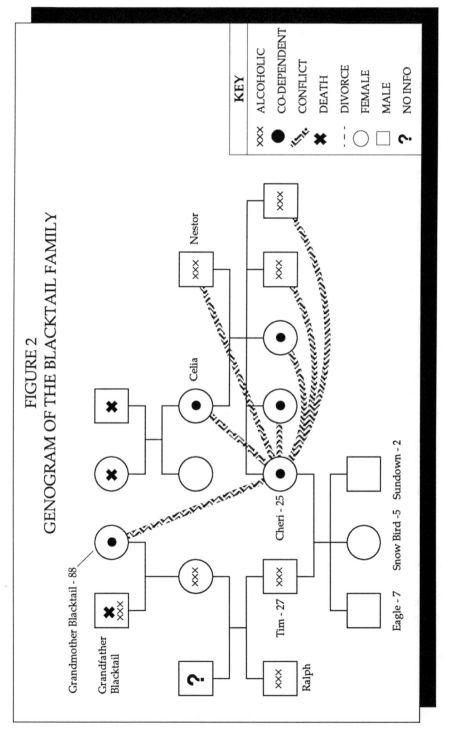

FIGURE 2
GENOGRAM OF THE BLACKTAIL FAMILY

71

Grandfather Blacktail was drunk, he beat them harshly, "to knock some sense into them," he said; and often they were black and blue for days. When they weren't physically abused, they were verbally abused. Tim became an alcoholic himself, starting his drinking at age ten. He would steal bottles from his grandfather when he was too drunk to notice or had passed out.

Ralph, did not use alcohol as a rule. His drug of choice was marijuana or cocaine. These substances were hard to get, and Ralph eventually left the Pueblo at age 13 and had not been heard of since. Tim didn't know if Ralph was alive or dead.

Tim dropped out of school in the ninth grade and could not hold down a job for more than a month at a time. His main source of income was drug dealing around the community. When he worked, it was as a laborer for local construction companies.

Cheri married Tim when she was just 17 years old. She also had dropped out of high school and was drinking and taking drugs with other teens in the nearby town. She never associated with the Indian kids of her community. Cheri was half Mexican. Her father was residing here illegally and had come to the U.S. to find work as a tilesetter. He was also a violent alcoholic, terrorizing his family for over 25 years. Cheri's mother was a tribal member, although Cheri's grandmother was of another tribe from another state. Cheri had two older sisters and two older brothers. When Cheri wasn't being physically beaten by her father, she was being emotionally abused by her older siblings.

The whole history of these two families was revealed in the first three-hour session held at Tim and Cheri's home. Also present were their three children, Eagle, age 7, Snow Bird, age 5, and Sundown, age 2.

The unique aspect about this case was that Tim had asked the therapist to help him and his family after attending a presentation she had conducted on dysfunctional families. This occurred while he was in detox at the tribal rehabilitation center.

The first session with the Blacktails occurred when Tim had just completed a 60-day treatment program and had been home for about two weeks. Although Tim had made his request for family intervention almost three months prior to this, the therapist and her clinical supervisor concurred that Tim needed to address his alcoholism first and that therapy with the family would not be successful if Tim was still "using."

During the course of two and a half years, the therapist became acquainted with the Blacktail's entire extended family.

Grandmother Blacktail:

Eighty-eight-year-old Phyllis Blacktail was the matriarch of the Blacktail family. She was severely crippled by arthritis and diabetes and was barely able to move around except in her own house. Although, she was in poor physical condition, she was still a very controlling and spiteful woman. Her only daughter had become an alcoholic and had left the village with a man twice her age. She rarely visited and kept up only minimal contact with her mother. However, Phyllis never spoke of her daughter's activities or lifestyle. She also never criticized or commented on the behavior of any of those close to her, especially not her husband, her daughter, or her two grandsons. Grandmother felt very close to Tim and she called upon him frequently to help her out. Therefore, she was hurt and angry when Tim married Cheri. She was quick to criticize and complain about Cheri and would go into a tirade about the shortcomings of Cheri, her family, other relatives, their children, tribal leaders, and everyone else in the community.

Cheri's Family :

Cheri was estranged from most of her family. Her mother and father lived in town but maintained the grandparents' house in the village, using it whenever they came to visit on weekends or on holidays.

Cheri's father, Nestor, had been a practicing alcoholic for more than 35 years. As a young boy, he was orphaned and physically abused by an uncle who kept him and made him work from dawn to sundown in a quarry digging for stone slate. Nestor was finally able to escape from his uncle with a group of men coming to the U.S. to work in the vegetable fields of Arizona. As a result of his childhood, Nestor was filled with hate and feelings of fear and abandonment. He also felt that he didn't belong in the U.S. but knew he could never return to his native country of Mexico. Nestor's use of alcohol made him forget these painful memories; and as he became a young man, he realized there were many things he'd rather forget.

Cheri's mother, Celia, also had feelings of insecurity and abandonment and unresolved feelings about her tribal heritage. She felt like she didn't belong anywhere. Her mother (Cheri's grandmother) was from a southeastern coastal tribe, and had second thoughts after marrying a handsome young soldier from New Mexico. She couldn't decide whether to remain with this man and adopt his people and his lifestyle in a state far from her own home or to remain at home in the south, close to familiar surroundings. Celia's father (Cheri's grandfather) came from a large family. He and his brothers were farmers; and when he returned from the war bringing home a family, he joined his brothers in their political strife over water rights. This historical conflict was between the Indian farmers and the non-Indians who farmed in the surrounding area.

Unfortunately, the farm slowly disappeared as Celia's parents struggled to stay together as a couple and keep the farm going. In the remaining years of their lives, they finally gave up on that notion, and Celia's mother returned to North Carolina, where she died of influenza. Celia's father remained on the farm, although nothing was left of it by then except the two-room house they had started with. He died within a year of his wife's death.

While Celia's parents tried to compromise on this issue, Celia and her sister spent 12 years in a government-run Indian boarding school in California. The boarding school was run in a strict militaristic fashion. Non-Indian "matrons" cared for the children in the dormitories, while other non-Indians provided the academic instruction. Throughout this ordeal, the children in the boarding school were not allowed to speak their native language or to practice any native rituals or traditions. In other words, they were stripped of all vestiges that made them Indians. Celia, like all the others, felt ashamed of being Indian, felt unloved, and wondered what was wrong with her. She especially wondered why her parents didn't want her.

Celia and Nestor married when she was 17 years old and he was 19. They had a large family consisting of two boys and three girls. Neither Celia nor Nestor had ever known the love of a parent or the stability of a familial household.

Needless to say, Cheri's brothers became alcoholics at young ages, married women who rescued them from their irresponsible behavior (co-dependents, by today's clinical definition), and were not unlike Cheri's sisters who married alcoholics. Each of these women heroically tried to keep her family fed, clothed, and with a roof overhead, despite the problems of alcoholism, family violence, unemployment, lack of skills and education.

Based on the extent of the dysfunction in both Cheri's and Tim's families of origin, there was a great deal to do in therapy.

The following were some of the issues the therapist focused on:

- Strengthening the marital bond, including assisting the couple to work through various intimacy issues.

- Establishing appropriate boundaries between the nuclear family and the extended family, which helped to strengthen Tim and Cheri's resolve to not become involved in their families' problems at this time.

Working with the extended family had not been part of the therapist's original plan of action. However, as the therapist's knowledge of the family grew, she was able to assess that many of Tim and Cheri's problems stemmed from learned behavior they grew up with from each of their families of origin. Furthermore, the therapist also discovered that the extended family had to be dealt with. Otherwise, Tim and Cheri would face eventual defeat in their battle to create a healthy family. Without the extended families' cooperation, all the efforts made by Tim, Cheri, and the therapist were in danger of being sabotaged by the rest of the family.

Example: " Why are you always coming around asking my Tim all kinds of questions about me?" Grandmother Blacktail asked the therapist.

The therapist replied: "Tim and Cheri have invited me to come see them. We're working on solving Tim's problems with alcohol, and they both have said that they want to be better parents to the children. I think I can help, but I would also like you to help me. I've asked Tim about you because you are important to him, and I think you know how I can be of help to Tim and Cheri and the children."

Cheri's family was more difficult to engage. Although Cheri wasn't especially close to anyone in her family, they all kept up on family antics via the family grapevine.

On the surface this tactic appears harmless and informal. However, in reality it was a very powerful controlling device used to keep family members in their problematic family roles.

Example: In the early stages of therapy, Cheri accompanied the therapist to a parent training class being held in the community. At the following therapy session, Cheri related this story to the therapist:

Cheri's sister Anita came to see her. "I just dropped by to give you these clothes that the kids aren't using anymore," said Anita. Did Mom tell you that D.J. and Jena (Cheri's brother and sister-in-law) are split? Well, I think it's great. Jena's always trying to make D.J. do dumb stuff. She invited the priest over to talk D.J. into going to a six-week marital retreat! Can you imagine? D.J. just laughed, said 'NO WAY' and offered him a beer! She's really dumb; I'm glad she's moving out."

For a long time Cheri was very fearful of her family finding out she and Tim were involved in family therapy. While she felt psychologically vulnerable, she avoided seeing her parents and other relatives.

- Providing basic skills in how to parent for both Tim and Cheri to assure that the children's physical and emotional needs were met. Issues that were discussed included appropriate disciplinary tactics, children's developmental stages, and the physical care and nurturing of children.

- Rendering necessary basic social services in the beginning. The family was given assistance in getting food stamps, general financial assistance from the BIA, referrals for employment services, and transportation to help Cheri set up a functional household.

As stated earlier, Tim and Cheri were seen consistently throughout a two-and-a-half year period. Eventually, Tim and Cheri became more involved in their community. Cheri was active in the Headstart program where the two youngest children attended school and also became a school board member at the day school where her oldest son was an honor student. Tim established a relationship with some of the tribal elders and was soon active in tribal ceremonies and community activities.

SUMMARY

The Native American community has concern for the individual and the family. Historically, the community used the power of this collective concern to shape behavior and strengthen values and morals of the group. Therapeutic intervention, drawing upon this inherent strength, can generate healthy, long-term changes for Indian families.

Home-Based Family Therapy is a model being used in many Indian communities across the United States. Current studies evaluating these programs have shown that some programs have been more successful than others. Therapists and program administrators need to communicate directly with each other about what works and what doesn't.

Obviously, more needs to be done to help strengthen existing programs and to promote the development of such programs in more Native American communities. Mental health agencies need to be open to using this model and to adopting the flexibility and creativity that is vital for HBFT to be successful.

REFERENCES

Ackerman, R. J. (1978). *Children of alcoholics: A guide book for educators, therapists, and parents.* Florida: Learning Publications, Inc.

Ackerman, R. J. (Ed.), (1986). *Growing up in the shadow: Children of alcoholics.* Florida: Health Communications, Inc.

Attneave, C. L. (1969). An analysis of therapeutic roles in tribal settings and urban network interventions. *Family Process,* 8, 192-210.

Black, C. (1981). *It will never happen to me.* New York: Ballentine Books.

Bradshaw, J. (1988). *Bradshaw: On the family, a revolutionary way of self-discovery. Healing the shame that binds you.* Florida: Health Communications, Inc.

Goodluck Tsoi, C. (1980). Strength and caring. *Journal of Contemporary Social Work,* 7, 519-521.

Hartman, A., & Laird, J. (1983). *Family-centered social work practice.* New York: The Free Press. Macmillan, Inc.

Helping Indian families. Prepared for Indian Family Defense. (1977). California: Association of American Indian Affairs. Urban Indian Child Resource Center.

Jilek, W. G. (1981). Anomic depression, alcoholism and a culture-congenial Indian response. *Journal of Studies on Alcohol,* Supp., No. 9, 159-170.

Jordan, J. (1987). Times have changed for Native Americans. *Changes,* July-Aug., 9.

Jordan, J., & Tafoya, N. (1989). Healing the dysfunctional family: A return to the sacred path. Presentation given at the Seventh Annual National American Indian Conference on Child Abuse and Neglect. Oregon.

Mannes, M., & Yuan, Y. T. (1988). Keeping Indian families together: The potential of family-based placement prevention services. Special Reprint, *American Indian Law Newsletter,* 21, 4/5, 20-47.

Middleton-Moz, J. (1986). The wisdom of the elders: Working with Native American and Native Alaskan families. In R. J. Ackerman (Ed.), *Growing up in the shadow : Children of alcoholics.* Florida: Health Communications, Inc.

Satir, V. (1972). *People making. Conjoint family therapy.* California: Science and Behavior Books, Inc.

Schacht, A., Tafoya, N., & Mirabal, K. (1989). Home-based therapy with American Indian families. *American Indian and Alaskan Native Mental Health Research*, 1, F.

Stanton, M.D. (1981). Marital therapy from a structural/strategic viewpoint. In G.P. Sholevar (Ed.), *Marriage is a family affair: A textbook of marriage and marital therapy.* New York: S.P. Medical and Scientific Books (Division of Spectrum Books).

Steinglass, P., Bennett, L., Wolin S., & Reiss, D. (1987). *The alcoholic family.* New York: Basic Books, Inc.

Wegsheider-Cruz, S. (1981). *Another chance: Hope and health for the alcoholic family.* California: Science and Behavioral Books, Inc.

Family Preservation Skills with Native Americans

JOHN P. RONNAU, JUNE C. LLOYD, ALVIN L. SALLEE,
AND PATRICIA J. SHANNON

INTRODUCTION

Competent and skilled teams of family preservation services (FPS) practitioners can effectively assist Native Americans to strengthen and preserve their families, thus providing a viable alternative to unnecessary family separations and out-of-home placements. FPS embody a philosophical approach that establishes the primacy of the family unit as the focal point of child welfare services. FPS are designed and delivered to support the child's family in reasserting its role in the development and socialization of its members. FPS are compatible with permanency planning objectives (A system 1986) because they encompass a range of activities designed to flexibly meet the needs of families with problems that threaten their stability. These activities may include case management, counseling/therapy, education/skill building, advocacy, and the provision of tangible services such as food, clothing, and housing (Family preservation 1985).

Both the goals and methods of the family preservation approach contribute to ethnically sensitive practice. According to Indian Child Welfare literature, "the family-based service philosophy and approach are compatible with the intent of the Indian Child Welfare Act and the desires of the Native Americans to preserve the integrity of Indian family life and traditions" (Family based 1982, p. 3). The family-based approach appears to have particular relevance for its adaptability to the numerous and varied cultural traditions represented among Native Americans (Family based 1982).

Family preservation services are most frequently provided by teams comprised of the family members themselves, professional and paraprofessional workers, and a variety of other resource persons in the community. Every effort should be made to have and train Native American personnel to provide family preservation services (Family based 1982). Since the ideal match between client system and workers is not always available, it is important that persons serving Native American families be trained in the skills necessary to make them effective and to avoid cultural damage. At the very least, one member of the team who shares the cultural/ethnic/racial heritage of the family should be able to serve as a cultural guide for the non-Indians.

VALUES AND PHILOSOPHY

Family preservation is first a philosophy about the essential role which families play in the welfare of children, what they need to do their job, and how they should be treated by service providers. As with any philosophy, it can only be put into practice when policies are established, funded, and implemented at the local level. Beyond program design, policy, and funding issues, implementation of family-centered practice requires the front line worker to have an *understanding and commitment* to the values and beliefs enumerated below.

The most prominent values which guide the implementation of the family preservation philosophy include: the belief that the family is the best environment for the growth and development of children, an overall purpose of family empowerment, the importance of meeting the family's basic needs, a commitment to cultural and ethnic sensitivity, and viewing client families as colleagues and members of the FPS team (Lloyd & Sallee in press).

The belief that the family is the best environment for the growth and development of children is paramount to the FPS approach. There is no bonafide substitute for the child's family of origin. FPS practitioners accept that in rare instances a child must be temporarily separated from the family for safety reasons. Even less frequently—for example, when the parent is severely disturbed—separations must be permanent. But the bias is clearly that families, ideally their own, are the best places for children.

Family preservationists do not see problems as lodging within individuals. For example, while the presenting problem may be a parent abusing alcohol or an out-of-control teenager, a worker using a systems approach would not limit attention to those behaviors. Instead, he/she would consider the entire family unit as a system in need of interactional modifications which lead to empowerment. Family preservation services address the needs of the entire family. In keeping with the emphasis on the importance of the family, no one member is singled out for intervention; instead, the family unit is the focus of services, and the needs of each member are addressed as a means of helping the entire family. The purpose of family preservation services is to empower families—not to diagnose, isolate, separate, or "straighten them out." Empowerment entails assisting each member, to the greatest extent possible, to contribute to the family's well-being.

Also underlying the family preservation approach is the belief that the entire community (the family, professionals, agencies and institutions) have a shared, interactional responsibility for strengthening and preserving families. Children are society's most important resource. Families play a critical and indispensable role in their development and growth. In accordance with that role, families deserve the community's unequivocal support and assistance.

Social workers who provide family focused services work from the traditional social work value base that asserts the dignity and worth of individuals, the individual's ability to grow and change, the responsibilities of individuals to help each other, and their responsibilities for achieving their highest potential. Social workers in a family focused delivery system also need to value the family, however, as an organizational unit, inherently capable of nurturing and teaching its members, and capable of positive growth and change as a system (Examining social work 1989, p. 103).

The family preservation perspective includes policies, services, and practices designed to strengthen and maintain the integrity of families while promoting the healthy growth and development of children. The family preservation approach focuses on delivering services to families rather than to individuals. The major objectives of FPS are: 1) to strengthen and maintain client families, 2) to prevent family dissolution and the placement of children out-of-home, and 3) to reduce client dependency on the social services system by promoting family self-sufficiency (Intensive family 1990). The underlying philosophical approach of family preservation, which establishes the primacy of the family as the focal point of child welfare services, is in keeping with Native American values.

The strength of commitment to families and the value base of family-centered services required of FPS practitioners necessitates equally strong supervisory and administrative support in order to sustain their efforts. FPS practitioners cannot survive for long in isolation. They require the direction and support of supervisors and like-minded colleagues to maintain this non-traditional approach to helping families.

CULTURAL COMPETENCE

Family preservation services draw heavily upon systems and ecological theories as frameworks for articulating ideal service delivery systems and interventions (Barth 1988). Consistent with those theories, a basic tenet of family-centered practice is that the helping process must occur within the family's natural setting (home, neighborhood, community, clan, tribe, and society). Individual family members are not worked with in isolation but instead are helped in relation to their significant others and their environment. These methods are more powerful in initiating change and vastly improve the chances of positive changes enduring.

Useful tools for obtaining an accurate picture of the family in context are the Eco-Map and Genogram (Bowen 1978; Hartman 1979; LeVine & Sallee 1986). Use of these tools almost always elicits new ideas for effective points of intervention from the family and other members of the FPS team. The Eco-Map is an excellent tool for visualizing and conceptualizing the forces and processes between the family and its environment. It can be used to illustrate the family's place in the community and its relationship to many other groups. Expanding the family's perceptions of their options often leads to feelings of increased optimism, power, and control. This mapping technique also allows for the charting of the directions and flow of resources, power, stress, and support. The results of these two information-gathering tools may be as complex as the family and worker choose to make them and may include much detail about extended family, clan, or tribal relationships. The information contained on the Genogram and Eco-Map can be a valuable aide for the non-Indian worker to gain an expanded perspective of the Native American family.

The family's cultural and ethnic heritage is an essential starting point for viewing the family within context. Workers should be "expected to understand and respect Indian cultural values and social norms and their intrinsic merit and inviolability. Protection of the Indian child includes the preservation and accessibility of the child's biological kinship system and culture" (Family based 1982, p. 3). Given the importance of values, rituals, and customs for the healthy functioning of Native American families, and the damage which has been done to them by insensitive and uninformed workers, it is important to stress the skill of cultural competence for the family preservation worker. Cultural competence is not an isolated technique used occasionally by the worker but is, instead, a value and set of skills which are woven into the entire helping process. Cultural sensitivities become doubly important when the work is done from the locus of the family's home.

A preliminary step in becoming a culturally competent worker is self-examination. The worker must possess the self-confidence and self-esteem to not be threatened by cultural differences. Instead, the culturally competent worker not only accepts differences but values and seeks them out as potential strengths for meeting the client's needs. In addition, culturally competent helping professionals:

- acknowledge cultural differences and become aware of how they affect the helping process.

- recognize the influence of their own culture on how they think and act.

- are aware of the effects of cross-cultural differences upon communication between worker and client.

- are conscious of the meaning of a client's behavior within his or her cultural context.

- can adjust the helping approach to utilize the client's cultural strengths. (Ronnau & Shannon 1990)

Becoming a culturally competent worker is a lifelong process. The more sensitive and aware one becomes, the more cultural differences are appreciated and valued as strengths. The process of becoming culturally competent includes the awareness that there is always more to learn about other cultures. A beginning point is to be aware and appreciate the implications of some of the major value differences between Native Americans and the dominant culture.

Too often child welfare workers have not understood or have ignored the power of family connections for Native Americans. Well-intentioned but culturally insensitive and biased service systems have aided in the systematic disruption of Indian family life. The effects are often devastating for Indian families, for "the trauma which results from separating children from family, culture, and community places the Indian child in triple jeopardy and removes a major motivating force in the lives of parents" (Family based 1982, p. 1).

When Indian families are subjected to intervention by workers who are not culturally competent, cultural bias and misunderstandings often influence the decision to place children. Material and spiritual values differ greatly between Indians and members of the dominant culture

(Family based 1982). Examples of major value differences between Native Americans and the dominant culture include:

- others before self **versus** putting self first,
- honoring your elders **versus** valuing youth,
- children belong to all **versus** children are the parent's property,
- few rules are best **versus** have a rule for everything, and
- simplify problems **versus** nothing is simple.
(Richardson 1981)

If the worker is not aware of these and other value differences and how they effect a person's view of the world, it is inevitable that communication will be difficult and misunderstandings will abound (Richardson 1981). It is important for child welfare workers to keep in mind "that theories regarding poverty and abuse and neglect in the general population are not appropriately superimposed upon the Indian" and that "tribal customs, religious practices and beliefs, traditions of social interaction, discipline, eating patterns, etc., are all susceptible to misunderstanding by the uninformed worker" (Family based 1982, p. 3).

The Indian way of thinking about children is so different from that of the dominant culture that it requires a willingness by the non-Indian worker to step back and view things from an entirely different perspective. From the Indian viewpoint, the child is more than just a child; he or she is a tribal person. "An American Indian child is born into two relational systems, a biological family and a kinship network, such as a clan or band" (Family based 1982, p. 3). Tribal membership is based on a mutual and interlocking relationship between individuals that is distinct from the non-Indian view of relationships; the concept of children as property is foreign. According to Indian values, a child has a right by virtue of birth to develop within the context of his or her culture and with the companionship of people through which the strongest definition of self can be formed.

SKILLS NEEDED FOR WORKING WITH NATIVE AMERICAN FAMILIES

Social work's generalist model of helping provides a useful framework for describing the skills needed by the family preservation worker to effectively serve Native American families. The description of skills is organized around the major components of the generalist helping model. Those are contact/relationship building, information gathering, assessment, implementation, evaluation, and termination (Sallee & Hoffman 1990).

Contact/Relationship Building

An important difference between traditional therapy and family-centered practice relationships is the latter's de-emphasis of the professional distance between workers and clients. The critical role which relationship plays in determining the effectiveness of the helping process has often been referred to in both the social work and family preservation literature (Compton & Galaway 1984; Lloyd & Bryce 1984; O'Neil 1984). In fact, the concept has been referred to so often that it is now taken for granted by many workers. This complacency regarding the importance of relationship is especially counterproductive when working with Native American families, given the values which many of them hold regarding self-reliance and non- interference.

Native Americans generally prefer to be self-reliant and may be hesitant to ask for or receive help. This self-reliance may incorrectly be interpreted by the worker as belligerence, stubbornness, or denial. This same characteristic may lead the American Indian to delay seeking help until it becomes absolutely necessary. The FPS practitioner should recognize this characteristic as a strength through which the process of empowerment may begin.

The worker should make use of all opportunities to identify and help the family make use of their strengths in ways that empower and engender trust. Avoiding criticism and judgments and, when possible, reframing problem behaviors as strengths can help to gain the family members' trust and confidence. The initial contacts by the FPS team may be the first time for many families that child welfare workers have acted as if they believed in the family's potentials to change and meet each others needs.

Most Native American groups consider interference in others' lives as a sign of disrespect. Their values are more in keeping with a "live and let live" philosophy. This preference may be in direct conflict with the worker's attempts to intervene in the family's life, actions which might be interpreted by Native Americans as disrespectful, threatening, or insulting.

The skills of active listening, empathy, and communication are important when initiating contacts and building relationships with Native Americans, as with all other clients. Of course, all contacts should be conducted in a respectful manner. This respect includes accepting cultural practices that the worker may not readily understand. For example, some Native American clients may prefer to hold meetings with the worker in the out-of-doors rather than in the confines of their dwelling. It is not unusual for more traditional Native Americans to offer food to the visitor. Accepting at least a small portion is a way of returning this sign of courtesy and respect.

The non-Indian worker should be aware that past experiences with the dominant society may have left a general distrust that will effect the level of trust which the Native American is willing to extend (Special issues 1989). Accordingly, the worker must be patient and realize that relationship building will take time.

Meeting with family members in the places where they are most comfortable, such as their home, is an important characteristic of the family preservation approach (Bryce & Lloyd 1981; Lloyd & Bryce 1984; Whittaker & Tracy 1988) and one especially pertinent to Native American clients. Their previous experiences with the child welfare system may leave them especially reluctant to meet with the worker in far removed and formal office settings.

Information Gathering

Skills required of the worker to effectively gather information include listening, and knowing who and what to ask when. Effective information gathering assumes that a relationship of trust and respect has been built with the client so that information will be shared. Whenever possible, the worker should begin the data collection process with open-ended, non-threatening questions as signs of respect for privacy, and a willingness to be patient. The Indian value of non-confrontation may lead the client to appear agreeable but refuse to comply when the worker is gone. It is important for the worker to understand that this is a difference in values and not a sign of belligerence or stubbornness.

Because of the community aspect of Native American lifestyles and values, the extended family is an important source of strength (Goodluck 1990). For example, all adult members of the family and community may serve in parental roles. Accordingly, the worker should interact not just with the parents but with other members of the family who are actively involved with the child's welfare when attempting to collect information or identify resources, assuming that confidentiality is respected. Workers should not make the mistake of searching only for formal resources, such as mental health professionals, but instead focus upon informal resources, such as family members and community.

Assessment

Investigation into the effectiveness of social work practice indicates that the process often is not helpful because the worker and the client are not working toward the same purposes (Compton & Galaway 1984). Effective assessment and planning require a partnership, or mutuality, between the worker and client. "Joint assessment and decision making is at the very heart of the development of the service contract" (Compton & Galaway 1984, p. 318). The family member's full participation in the assessment of strengths, concerns, needs, available and needed resources, and planning for action requires that a trusting and positive working relationship has been established. FPS practitioners attempt to acknowledge and underscore this by conceptualizing the family/worker partnership (system) as requiring joint involvement in each of the four components of the assessment process. Assessment is defined as both a statement and process which makes sense of the information collected (Sallee & Hoffman 1990). The FPS team's assessment should include four components: 1) how the area of strengths and concern are defined and by whom; 2) how the use of systems theory helps to select and create interventions; 3) what changes need to occur and how the team will catalyze, facilitate, and initiate the change; and 4) what informal and formal resources must be obtained (Siporin 1975; Sallee & Hoffman 1990). While assessment, planning, and contracting are closely tied together, they are not one and the same. An accurate and pertinent assessment of the family's strengths and needs will identify where change needs to occur. An effective assessment will help the FPS team design a useful plan which in turn will make implementation go far more smoothly and effectively (Sallee & Hoffman 1990). Labeling and its negative consequences should be avoided during the assessment processes.

A basic FPS tenet is that many families (already frightened and angered by the traditional Child Protection System process) are confused and powerless in the face of legal, medical, educational, mental health and other professional culture mind sets and jargon. One key to making the assessment process positive and useful is to focus on the strengths of the family. This strengths or family empowerment focus is a hallmark of the family preservation approach. It is also important to clarify the mind sets and jargon of other team members in the family's presence and get providers to conceptualize their roles in the family's terminology. The beginning of the empowerment process is to effectively assist the family in sharing information and understanding their needs and strengths.

The family empowerment process recognizes and emphasizes the strengths and positive potential of the family while not denying needs or concerns. Believing in the potential of the family to deal with its concerns and needs and encouraging hope within the family are examples of the strengths approach (Examining social work 1989). As an example of empowerment, identifying and engaging persons with expertise which the family can trust (e.g., respected tribal leaders, tribal elders, Native American professionals or paraprofessionals, and cultural guides) will help to clarify and assist with developing problem definitions and options for their resolution which the family can support. Use of the strengths approach does not justify a denial of problems; the difference from traditional methods is that the strengths of the family are more zealously assessed than weaknesses, and strengths become the primary means for resolving problems. Furthermore, reframing problem behaviors as strengths whenever possible provides fresh perspectives which are valuable to the entire FPS team (Lloyd & Sallee in press).

Skills required of the worker to carry out the assessment process include listening, collaborating with the family and the system with which they are involved, and assisting the family to prioritize. Making the clients an integral part of the assessment process requires that their trust and confidence have been earned. An obvious but important step which must be taken is for the worker to ask family members what they need to resolve their concerns, what has already been tried, and what they feel the priorities should be. Most clients, especially Native Americans who have had negative contacts with the dominant culture child welfare system, may be reluctant to openly state their opinions. This reluctance is understandable and requires patience on the worker's part.

Recognizing the family in context includes having knowledge of its cultural and ethnic heritage. The implications of viewing the family within that cultural context means that 1) their strengths are more readily identified; 2) the relevant systems, key people in the family, and possible intervention points are all more readily discovered; and 3) specific knowledge can be gained about such questions as: what symbols are meaningful to family members, how they define health and mental health, and how their primary support networks are configured (Cultural competence 1988).

The time-limited nature of the family preservation approach (usually no more than one to three months) raises serious concerns about the non-Indian's ability to establish the level of trust and rapport necessary to effectively help Native Americans. FPS team members must be aware that the time frame for providing the family preservation service may need to be lengthened to allow for trust to develop. If the non-Indian is to be at all effective in such a short time, cultural competence becomes even more critical. The importance of Native American team members and/or cultural guides being available cannot be overemphasized.

Family preservationists can also help to improve the child welfare risk assessment process. Their values, philosophy toward families, systemic viewpoint, and skills predispose them to be competent risk assessors. In those instances in which children must be removed from their families, either temporarily or permanently, the family preservation team can provide invaluable observations and assistance. The extensive and intensive work with the family inherent in the FPS approach allows for accurate identification and documentation over time of those situations which truly do place children at risk. This intensive team involvement can also provide alternative plans for the child's safety with as much family involvement as possible.

Planning

The activities for planning to achieve desired changes cannot be artificially separated from the other stages of the FPS approach. Advanced family preservation practitioners simply do not view the stages as chronologically separate, but systematically simultaneous and ongoing. Ideally, plans will not be formulated until information collection and assessment activities have been thoroughly completed. However, in order to meet the needs of families in crisis and to capture the therapeutic openings which crises represent, planning activities may need to occur as early as the first contact. In any case, the collection of information, assessment, and planning is an integrated and ongoing process.

Planning for effective action requires a positive working relationship characterized by openness and mutuality among all members of the team. It is especially important that the family members who are the recipients of the FPS service feel a part of the planning process and can sincerely "own" the results. Unless the clients for whom the plan is developed understand its importance and perceive the potential benefits to them, it is unlikely that it will be successfully carried out.

Again, the skills of active listening and being able to ask non-threatening but useful questions are important for the FPS worker. Especially during planning activities, team-building skills such as encouraging involvement, preventing domination by one member of the team, being sure all members feel comfortable enough to participate, and assisting members to reach a consensus are important (Hooyman 1979; Simons

1982). The ability to help team members formulate realistic, clear, and achievable objectives is another obvious but essential skill.

It is important for the worker to keep in mind that some Native American clients will be reluctant to play an active role in planning for change unless trust, respect, and acceptance are in evidence from other team members. Building such an atmosphere may take even more time if the worker is not Native American.

Implementation of the Case Plan

As needed information is collected and sorted and strengths assessed and concerns prioritized, the worker and family together implement the case plan for action. In keeping with the systemic nature of the FPS approach, implementation occurs simultaneously and continually along with other components of the helping process. When implementing plans of action which have been agreed upon by the FPS team, the workers are challenged to use their abilities, skills, knowledge, and contacts to assist the clients to reach their mutually defined goals (Compton & Galaway 1984).

Skills required of the worker to implement the action plan include listening, communication, coalition building, creativity, flexibility, and staying focused. It may also be helpful for the worker to think about the implementation stage of the helping process as involving one or more (depending on the family's needs) of the following roles: broker, enabler, teacher, mediator, advocate (Compton & Galaway 1984).

An additional key FPS practitioner role is that of coordination. Coordination includes role delineation, joint goals, and a common frame of reference. Coordinating multiple services requires that the worker be able to plan with the entire FPS team, including family members, and bring them together effectively for joint sessions. Ideally, the worker will model for and coach the family to assume an active role in the coordination process and, eventually, to learn to direct it themselves. Teaming with other agencies on behalf of the family requires that the worker have the skills to encourage open communication, build respect, and initiate joint decision making. In order to avoid the potential damage caused to the family by long-term exposure to fragmented, uncoordinated services, the FPS worker must develop a sense of timing and make use of windows of opportunity opened by crises.

As a broker of services, the worker attempts to make connections between the clients and the formal and informal resources which they need. With Native American people, the worker's first recourse should be to attempt to connect the clients to informal resources such as family, friends, or other members of the community. An Indian family in need of temporary care for their children after a neglect incident, for example, is best served if other family members can help, rather than by having them placed with strangers in a group home.

In the role of enabler, the worker helps family members to identify and use the strengths and resources within themselves needed to make desired changes. As an enabler, the worker relies heavily upon the strengths which have been identified within the family and assists family members to use these strengths to meet their needs. Providing hope and encouragement and expressing faith in the family's potential to solve its problems is an important aspect of this role. A family struggling with alcohol abuse may need a great deal of encouragement and reinforcement for tackling the problem, in addition to being connected to formal and informal community services.

As a teacher, the worker may provide the family with needed information for resolving concerns, model alternative ways to interact, or assist clients to practice new behaviors. Parents of a child with emotional problems may never have been provided specific alternatives for responding to a youth's troublesome tantrums, so that their only recourse is physical punishment. The worker also can help by providing accurate and usable information about the child's emotional problems. In this role it is particularly important to be able to identify the cognitive and cultural variations in how family members receive information, process it, and learn.

In the role of mediator, the worker helps to resolve disputes which may occur between family members and other persons or organizations. As an advocate, the worker represents or argues for the clients' needs in order to help meet their goals. It is not unusual for non-Indian members of the formal child welfare system to misinterpret a parent's reliance upon extended family members for child care as a sign of neglect. As a mediator, the family preservation worker interprets this behavior to other team members as normal and healthy family interdependence among Native Americans.

Evaluation

Good intentions and a desire to help are not enough. Workers have an obligation and responsibility to continuously monitor the effectiveness of their helping efforts. Measures must be taken to ensure that the clients are "getting their money's worth" from the service being provided.

Evaluation skills required of the worker include regular and consistent monitoring of progress towards achieving the clients' goals from the outset and, of course, the ability to communicate with the clients to obtain their opinions about the progress being made.

Evaluation is an ongoing process which requires that realistic, measurable, and achievable goals have been mutually agreed upon by the clients and worker and that methods of documentation are culturally acceptable. In turn, the goals can only be reached if objectives which meet the same standards have been identified. Useful goals and objectives provide a logical and meaningful focus for evaluation. Native American values, such as non-confrontation and non-interference, will present an added challenge to the evaluation process. The culturally competent worker will provide a variety of non-threatening means for the clients to provide feedback about their satisfaction with the service being provided.

Ending Phase

Especially in the time-limited family preservation approach, ending the helping relationship is an important part of the helping process and begins at the first contact with the clients. It is during that first meeting that the worker clarifies the time-limited nature of the team's work with the family. Skills required of the worker to complete the termination process include communication, empathy, and congruence.

It is important that a service such as FPS, which encompasses broader systems, includes building in supports to maintain the changes which have occurred in the family system. Much good work will be wasted if no thought is given or action taken to anticipate difficulties which could lead to back-sliding or relapses.

Toward the end of the termination process, the worker reviews with the clients the progress made. Much credit should be given to family members for their successes. The forms which rewards, celebrations, or acknowledgments take must be respectful and culturally sensitive. It is also important to be clear and direct about what work remains to be done and goals that were not accomplished.

At the time of the last contacts between the worker and clients, a mix of feelings can be expected. Not infrequently, families create crises due to termination anxiety. Some families may be relieved to have the worker out of their lives, at last. If the worker has been effective in establishing positive working relationships, there may be some mixture of sadness and regret. The worker's feelings about termination can be shared to a degree appropriate with the client's comfort level; while Native American clients may be asked to do the same, their reluctance to do so should be respected.

CASE EXAMPLE AND APPLICATION

This case example is based upon the actual experience of a young Native American couple. A sufficient number of details were changed to protect their identity. This story is told here to serve as an example of *harmful child welfare practices* with Native American families. Following the case example positive alternatives for helping this family from the FPS approach are discussed.

Laura and Frank had moved from their beautiful and serene home on the pueblo to a major Southwest urban center. The family's plans were for Frank to enroll in specialized training in auto mechanics while Laura worked to supplement the family's income, since the tribal scholarship funds were limited and not sufficient to meet their needs. While in reality they were only two hours away from home and family, it seemed like a million miles to them.

Feelings of isolation and despair escalated for the young couple frustrated by car trouble, a too small apartment, a three-month-old baby, and the crowded city. The pressures were building within Frank and came to a head one evening when Laura was away at her waitressing job. She stuck with the late night work schedule in order to avoid having to place the infant, Sara, in day care. Frank was finding it difficult to concentrate on studying while caring for the baby. The class work was frustrating and confusing to him. Making matters worse, his previous experience with child care was virtually nil. At home, both Frank's and Laura's parents and grandparents had made significant contributions to caring for their children. But now, these tried and trusted resources were not available to them.

On this particular Friday night, with a major test looming on the horizon for Saturday morning, Frank left the baby alone a few minutes to buy a six pack of beer. He rarely drank but was desperate for some help to relax and forget his loneliness for awhile. He returned to find Sara crying and despite his best efforts she would not stop. All his walking, talking, attempts to feed her and check for wet diapers had no effect. His anxiety about the pending test and need for study time lowered his frustration tolerance to the breaking point. He began to violently shake Sara and squeeze her arms tightly which, of course, only caused her to protest even more loudly.

93

Laura, with her own frustrations and fatigue, returned home to this frightening and troubling scene. Never had she seen her husband intoxicated, though she had too often observed the damaging effects of alcohol in others. Those fears and anxieties, coupled with the bruises she saw on her baby's arms, made her almost hysterical. She ran from the apartment and sought the help of neighbors who convinced her to call the State Human Services Department (HSD). She had a vague hope that the state workers might help since she knew the Indian social worker at home and liked her.

Unfortunately, the outcome was anything but positive when the HSD investigator arrived. From the culturally incompetent, non-Indian's viewpoint the worker observed a chaotic and confused situation with a "drunk Indian" and a bruised baby. Sara was taken into emergency custody, while Laura and Frank were left alone with their hurt, confusion, and bewilderment. The worker informed them that they would be contacted on Monday.

Anxious to see their daughter as soon as possible, Frank and Laura attended the "show cause hearing" on Monday as instructed. They were rudely confronted by a strange and foreign courtroom atmosphere, with only non-Indians in attendance, and an order granting temporary custody of their daughter to HSD. A service plan was dictated to the couple which mandated Frank into treatment for alcohol abuse and forbade the couple from contact, requiring Laura to move into an apartment on her own.

Despite Laura's desperate yearning to return to family for comfort and advice, she dared not leave the city and miss her once per week opportunities to visit her daughter in the social worker's office. Sara's father was not allowed to visit at all. While Laura knew her daughter was in foster care, the non-Indian foster mother would not allow parents to visit.

The consequences of this well-intentioned but dreadfully harmful intervention were many. Sara was nine months old before she was returned to her parents. Frank and Laura's relationship was virtually destroyed. He returned to the pueblo in shame, while Laura stayed in the city to maintain her job.

In retrospect, Laura described herself as being frightened and in shock when her baby was removed. The social worker's case records only described her as "angry, uncooperative, and sullen." Several times she was threatened with eviction for failure to pay rent. Laura was placed in a no-win situation by the HSD service plan. Her natural self-reliance and determination were interpreted as belligerence and stubbornness by the non-Indian workers. But eventually, her gentle caring ways with Sara

94

won the social workers' hearts.

There were no family preservation services or trained workers in this large metropolitan office. The workers lack of awareness and training, coupled with excessive caseloads, made them insensitive and short-sighted. As a consequence, a child was "protected"; but an Indian family was destroyed.

Application of the Family Preservation Approach

A very different scenario would have occurred had Frank, Laura, and Sara been assisted by a family preservation worker. At the outset, the goal of service would be to strengthen and preserve the family and prevent an out-of-home placement.

During the initial crisis phase, the worker would include the following questions in his/her information gathering:

1. Are family members within helping distance? Can another family member come to stay with the young couple until the crisis subsides?

2. Does Frank have a history of alcohol abuse or was this an isolated incident due to stress? Is there a history of family violence?

3. Could Frank be removed for a weekend "cooling off" period, leaving the developmentally vulnerable young child with her mother?

4. Could mother and child find somewhere to stay for the weekend?

5. Could mother and child together be placed in temporary care until the assessment is completed?

Only as a last resort would the child be placed in care away from her parents. A positive assessment, based on any of the five alternatives, would have allowed Sara to remain with one of her parents. Instead, she suffered the trauma of separation and entered a foreign world for six of the developmentally most critical months of her young life (Clarke-Stewart & Koch 1983; Newman & Newman 1984; Zastrow & Kirst-Ashman 1987).

This young mother was in crisis and reached out in desperation to social workers for help because of the trust she had previously learned. A culturally competent worker would first and foremost assess the family's strengths and realize that this was a young Native American couple in new and unfamiliar surroundings, away from family and friends for the first time.

A plan for some practical concrete services could have helped the family quickly regain balance. Sufficient money so that Laura would not have to work, transportation assistance, and tutoring to relieve Frank's anxiety are a few examples. Connections should have been made immediately to the local urban Indian center. Resources in the family's neighborhood or apartment complex could have been tapped for child care. Perhaps there were many other parents experiencing similar demands and in need of cooperative childcare assistance. Homemaker-helpers could have assisted the parents with their responsibilities and subsequently would have observed them to be competent loving parents. Those same homemakers could have taught Frank the skills to care for his daughter. Attempts should have been made immediately to contact family members back home to request help and support, including someone to come to the city and help with child care. At the same time, the option for Laura to temporarily return home with the baby could have been explored.

Not only were these practical services overlooked, but in addition, no service plan was mutually developed with the couple, no Indian staff or cultural guides were consulted, and no attempts were made to connect with the rich network of family and tribe inherently available to many Native Americans. A wide variety of intensive, immediate, and culturally sensitive services (all of which are characteristics of the FPS service approach) could have prevented Sara's separation from her parents, the father's shame, and the mother's many losses and grief.

CONCLUSION

Family preservation services are designed to place the family at the center of the helping process and foster a team approach. From a systems perspective, family preservation workers identify formal and informal resources needed by the family. Family members themselves become critical to the family preservation team. Emphasis is placed upon looking for and using the family's strengths in order to resolve its concerns.

A family's cultural and ethnic heritage is a prominent starting point from which to explore its strengths. This heritage is an especially valuable resource for Native American families. In order for family preservation workers to be effective helpers, they must be culturally competent. Cultural competence includes having a knowledge of the significant value differences between the dominant culture and Native

Americans and the important role which clan and tribal identity play in their lives. The worker must also develop a thorough knowledge and awareness of his/her own values, along with their impacts upon behavior and communication.

Contact/relationship building, information gathering, assessment, planning, implementation, and evaluation are the major skills needed by the family preservation practitioner. These skills, implemented with Native American families by culturally competent professional and paraprofessional workers, can prevent unnecessary out-of-home placements and help to preserve the Native American child's most important resource—its family.

REFERENCES

A system of care for severely emotionally disturbed children and youth. (1986). Task Force on Emotionally Disturbed Youth for the Division of Children and Family Services. Arkansas: Arkansas Department of Human Services.

Barth, R. P. (1988). Theories guiding home-based intensive family preservation services. In J. Whittaker, J. Kinney, E. Tracy, & C. Booth (Eds.), *Improving practice technology for work with high risk families: Lessons from the homebuilders social work education project.* Washington: Center for Social Welfare Research, School of Social Work, University of Washington.

Bowen, M. (1978). *Family therapy in clinical practice.* New York: Jason Aronson, Inc.

Bryce, M., & Lloyd, J. C. (Eds.) (1981). *Treating families in the home: An alternative to placement.* Illinois: Charles C. Thomas.

Clarke-Stewart, A., & Koch, J. B. (1983). *Children: Development through adolescence.* New York: John Wiley & Sons.

Compton, B., & Galaway, B. (1984). *Social work processes.* Illinois: The Dorsey Press.

Cultural competence continuum. (1988). *Focal Point, 3,* 1. Oregon: Portland State University, Research and Training Center, Regional Research Institute for Human Services.

Examining social work curriculum in the perspective of current practice with children and families. (1989). *Collaboration for competency.* Kentucky: University of Kentucky.

Family based services and the Native American. (1982). Iowa: National Resource Center on Family Based Services, University of Iowa.

Family preservation services. (1985). New York: Child Welfare League of America.

Goodluck, Tsoi C. (1990). Mental health issues of Native American transracial adoptions. In P. V. Grabe (Ed.), *Adoption resources for mental health professionals.* New Jersey: Transaction Publishers.

Hartman, A. (1979). *Finding families: An ecological approach to family assessment in adoption.* California: Sage Publications, Inc.

Hooyman, G. (1979). Team building in the human services. In B. Compton & B. Galaway (Eds.), *Social work processes.* Illinois: The Dorsey Press.

Intensive family services implementation guidelines. (1990). Publication 80. Arkansas: Arkansas Department of Human Services.

LeVine, E., & Sallee, A. (1986). *Listen to our children.* Iowa: Kendall/Hunt Publishing Company.

Lloyd, J. C. (1984). *Basic family-centered curriculum for family service workers and parent aides.* Iowa: National Resource Center on Family Based Services, University of Iowa.

Lloyd, J. C., & Bryce, M. E. (1984). *Placement prevention and family reunification: A handbook for the family-centered service practitioner.* Iowa: National Resource Center for Family Based Services, University of Iowa.

Lloyd, J. C., & Sallee, A. (in press). *Selected proceedings from the third annual empowering families conference in Charlotte, North Carolina.* National Association of Family Based Services.

Maluccio, A. N. (1988). Family-based services and public policy: Context and implications. In J. K. Whittaker, J. Kinney, E. M. Tracy, &

C. Booth (Eds.), *Improving practice technology for work with high risk families: Lessons from the homebuilders social work education project.* Washington: Center for Social Welfare Research, University of Washington.

Newman, B. M., & Newman, P. R. (1984). *Development through life: A psychosocial approach.* Illinois: The Dorsey Press.

O'Neil, M. J. (1984). *The general method of social work practice.* New Jersey: Prentice-Hall, Inc.

Richardson, E. H. (1981). Cultural and historical perspectives in counseling American Indians. In D. W. Sue (Ed.), *Counseling the culturally different.* New York: John Wiley & Sons.

Ronnau, J., & Shannon, P. (1990). A strengths approach to helping Native American families. *Indian Child Welfare Digest,* Feb./Mar. Oklahoma: Three Feathers Associates.

Sallee, A., & Hoffman, K. (1990). A follow-up study of BSW social workers: Implications for generalist education and practice. A paper presented at the 36th Annual Program Meeting, CSWE, Reno, Nevada, Mar. 3-6.

Simons, R. L. (1982). Strategies for exercising influence. *Social Work, 33,* May, 268-274.

Siporin, M. (1975). *Introduction to social work practice.* New York: Macmillan Publishing Co., Inc.

Special issues for foster care parents. (1989). *Indian Child Welfare Digest,* Oct./Nov. Oklahoma: Three Feathers Associates.

Whittaker, J. K., & Tracy, E. M. (1988). Family preservation services and education for social work practice: Stimulus and response. In J. K. Whittaker, J. Kinney, E. M. Tracy, & C. Booth (Eds.), *Improving practice technology for work with high risk families: Lessons from the homebuilders social work education project.* Washington: Center for Social Welfare Research, University of Washington.

Zastrow, C., & Kirst-Ashman, K. (1987). *Understanding human behavior and the social environment.* Illinois: Nelson-Hall Publishers.

The Role of Program Evaluation in the Development and Assessment of Family Preservation Services for American Indians and Alaskan Natives

YING-YING T. YUAN

INTRODUCTION

The Usefulness of Evaluation

Increasingly, program evaluation is considered an important part of program development and implementation. Recent specifications for conducting demonstration programs have included requirements that such programs be internally evaluated and, in some instances, participate in an external evaluation (Office of Human Development Services 1990).

Evaluation is commonly defined as the process by which we can determine the value or worth of something. Program evaluation consists of gaining an understanding of the implementation and outcomes of programs in order that we can improve services to children and their families. Typically, an evaluation addresses the following general questions (Yuan & Rivest 1990).

- What are the characteristics of the program administration and design?
- Does the program meet its stated goals and objectives?
- What clients are served by the program?
- What resources are expended in providing services?
- What services are provided?
- What are the outcomes of the services?
- What is the cost of the services?

Another way of stating these questions is from the perspective of the program providers. Are we being more successful with families this year? How do we define success? How can we improve our program design? What client outcomes are being achieved. Do we use resources efficiently?

In looking at such questions, an evaluation can focus on different stages of program implementation. Evaluations which focus primarily on the implementation process are often called process or formative evaluations; studies which focus primarily on the effects of services on those who receive them are commonly called outcome or summative evaluations.

A formative evaluation looks at the early stages of program development. At this point, little may be known about the results of the program; but much can be learned about the goals and objectives of the program, how well these statements are defined, how well the target population is defined, and what coordination is needed in order to develop the program.

A summative evaluation examines what happens to clients who receive services. What happened to the clients who were served? Did the program reach its objectives? Did clients improve or attain the stated objectives? Summative evaluations examine efficiency issues as well as effectiveness issues. An efficiency evaluation looks at the costs of providing the services, whether resources are well used, whether there are savings resulting from the program, etc.

Program evaluation addresses these questions for different reasons. Program managers may need to know how to allocate and plan their staff resources. Departmental directors want to know how may unduplicated clients are being served by each program and whether a small number of families use a large number of services on a chronic basis. Advocates for families need data to convince tribal council members, elders, and/or legislators to fund innovative and effective programs. In addition to meeting funding requirements, there are several potential benefits to conducting evaluations which are meaningful to the community:

- Additional funding may be provided

- Limited resources may be better allocated and targeted

- Increased effectiveness of program design may decrease the length of time clients depend upon programs

- Increased understanding of a program's requirements may refine staffing requirements

- Improved services may be able to break the cyclical nature of family and social problems

Barriers to Achieving the Potential Benefits of Evaluation

One of the major barriers to achieving the potential of evaluation activities is the failure to recognize that evaluation is a "culturally bound activity."

> Situational responsiveness begins with the recognition that evaluation is a culturally bound activity. Evaluation research is a subcultural perspective and set of practices within the larger culture of science. Program staff and clients will vary in the extent to which they understand and share the empirical orientation that is central to scientific cultures and subcultures. Given this variation, every evaluation becomes a cross-cultural encounter—a blending or confrontation between culturally different perspectives represented by evaluators and program staff or participants (Patton 1985, p.94).

The cultural parameters impacting evaluation designs and objectives include not only methodological differences among researchers and different orientations held by evaluators and program managers but also, and perhaps most importantly, cultural variations among different groups. Merryfield (1985) identifies three major areas of impact related to cross-cultural evaluation endeavors:

1. Cultural differences, including beliefs and values, styles of interaction, sense of time, infrastructure, and language

2. Methodological differences, including use of standardized measures, the scientific method, and data collection techniques

3. Ethical issues, including politicalization and evaluation, cultural imperialism, responsibility to the community and clients, and protection of data sources

Each of these areas can impact the evaluation design and implementation and analysis of data.

Another major barrier is that evaluative studies often impose extra burdens upon service delivery staff without providing them with any additional information. Redundant data may be asked for without consultation with staff or managers as to what information they need to better run their programs. For tribes and Indian nonprofits, where there is a severe lack of resources, this is a significant barrier to effective evaluations.

To address these barriers, some basic premises need to be established. An initial set of premises is stated below.

• Cultural values must be taken into account when designing programs and methods to evaluate such programs.

• Evaluation objectives should be selected which meet the needs of the American Indian community.

• Evaluation objectives should be negotiated with service providers as well as with the other potential users of data.

• Evaluation should answer questions or address issues of concern to the direct service staff as well as to management.

• Feedback based upon analysis of data should be provided at timely intervals.

• The burden upon direct service staff for data collection should be minimized. This means that data collection forms should serve multiple functions (e.g., case record management and evaluation).

In this article, cultural variables which may need to be considered when implementing and evaluating family preservation services are presented, and a case record approach for collecting data for both case management and evaluation is suggested. Areas of data collection which will require further discussion and review are identified.

CULTURAL FOUNDATIONS

Several articles in this volume have discussed different components of traditional value systems which may be important for consideration.

Horejsi (1989 A) in conjunction with representatives from several tribes has also discussed "generalizations about both the dominant society and the traditional Native American cultures." In his discussion, he includes such topics as the meaning of time, competition among people, control, definition of self, social interaction, material possessions, personal space, individual freedom, learning process, family, children, elders, religion, and spirituality. Examples of some of the contrasts which he presents are given below. Some of the examples are particularly relevant to implementing and evaluating family preservation services.

The Meaning of Time
(Contemporary U.S. Society) Time is measured by clock and calendar. Schedules, deadlines, time management, and saving time are all important. Emphasis is on planning the future so it can be "controlled." "Time is money." To "waste" someone's time is an offensive and rude behavior. Man is in a "race with time." There is never enough time to get done all that needs to be done.

(Traditional Native American) There is less preoccupation with time and planning, more emphasis on living from day to day. "Time is a gift from the Creator—an opportunity to discover your life's purpose and experience creation." (Traditionally, time was measured by natural events, e.g., sunrise, first snow, seasons of the year, etc.) Having patience, showing respect, and caring for others is of more importance than being "on time" as measured by a clock. To break off a discussion in order to keep another appointment is offensive and rude behavior.

Control
(Contemporary U.S. Society) Much emphasis on gaining control of people, things, and nature. Terms such as "intervention," "planning," and "strategy" reflect the desire to be in control. There are some ambivalent feelings about manipulation of people, but it is seen as necessary "in order to get things done." Man should attempt to improve on the natural state.

(Traditional Native American) Emphasis is on living in unison with and adapting to others and to nature. To try to control or manipulate others is viewed as rude and offensive behavior. There is reluctance to interfere in the lives of other people and strong feeling of resentment toward those that attempt to impose their will. There is a tendency toward fatalism, i.e., "What is meant to happen will happen and you

104

cannot and should not try to change it." Persons outside the culture interpret this as passivity.

Social Interaction

(Contemporary U.S. Society) Assertiveness, directness, eye contact, and a firm handshake are signs of a confident, trustworthy person. The hail and hardy, joking, outgoing, back-slapping individual is admired. Business seeks out the "can do" and "aggressive" individual. Making some enemies is seen as necessary in the "climb to the top." Being a "self starter" and desiring to assume a leadership role are valued qualities.

(Traditional Native American) Directness and assertiveness are offensive behaviors. In interpersonal relations, the individual is to be patient, humble, quiet, and especially respectful toward older people. Great emphasis is placed on maintaining interpersonal harmony, especially within the extended family.

Learning Process

(Contemporary U.S. Society) Emphasis is on formal education, the ability to conceptualize, empiricism, and the scientific method. Degrees, certification, and other credentials are important in establishing credibility. Emphasis is on careful selection and structuring of a child's experiences and activities so the child will reach certain "learning objectives."

(Traditional Native American) Emphasis is on learning by doing and by watching others (modeling). Intuition and life experience are valued. Children are given considerable freedom so they will learn from the consequences (both positive and negative) of their decisions and behavior. Limit setting is rare in child rearing.

Defining the Family for Family Preservation Services

The definition of the term "family" is perhaps one of the fundamental concepts which need consideration when designing and evaluating services. In some programs, although the term "family" is used, the focus of the service is actually the mother and child; in other programs it includes all members of the extended family who live in the same household; in still others it includes an approach which involves selected kin or all kin who live in the area. "Family" may also include non-relatives who have assumed the role of kinsmen. Among many tribes, the term would be more encompassing than that of the average Caucasian "family" receiving social services. Social workers who are not experienced in American Indian culture may encounter grandparents, uncles, aunts, and cousins who assume and perform roles which the social workers find difficult to understand. Decisions may be the product of a group rather than an individual.

Services which are family preservation will need to define what is meant by "family". A more inclusive definition may require that different types of instruments are used to measure family functioning. Certainly, both practice and evaluation might be more complex because of the range of individuals who are involved in the intervention.

Defining Placement

Another critical area of attention is the definition of "placement." One of the major policy goals of family preservation services, as applied in child welfare and mental health services, is to provide an alternative to removing a child from his/her home. Family-based services, especially when provided intensively, constitute one approach for increasing the chances of a child to remain "at home." In American Indian and Alaskan Native communities, with the likelihood of a wider definition of family and home and a recognition of the importance of placing children with relatives and other tribal members, which placements are to be averted and which placements are to be considered as living with other relatives but not being "placed?" What will be the definition of "placed?" (See Plantz, Hubbell, Barrett, & Dobrec 1988.) Should all placements be considered ones to be avoided, or only those which place children in non-relative homes? One solution, which considers a placement as any living arrangement which is paid for by child welfare funds, may not be acceptable to the culture.

Service Model Options

A third area which needs to be defined is the service model itself. The new standards developed by the Child Welfare League of America include the following services as those which strengthen and preserve families (CWLA 1989):

Family Resource, Support and Education Services include informal support to participants, parent education, peer support groups and peer counseling, recreation services, early developmental screening, enhancement of child development, child day care services, home visits, referral and linkage to appropriate resources, and outreach. Services are not time limited.

Family-Centered Casework Services include case management, counseling/therapy, education/skill building, advocacy and/or provision of concrete services such as food, housing, or health care, with caseloads of about 15 families per worker for a period of six months or longer.

Intensive Family-Centered Crisis Services provide intensive counseling, education, and support services to families in serious crisis, with caseloads of two to 12 families for a period of four to 12 weeks.

This framework of services has some important implications for evaluative studies. First, it presumes that these models are found to be unique and separate in the service delivery system. In communities where services are not fragmented among multiple providers, it may be difficult to separate out each of the services. The worker who is providing intensive family-centered crisis services may also be the worker who would provide less intensive services and who runs the recreation program. Second, the goals of each of the services may be specified in similar terms. For example, all of the programs might have the goals of preventing the removal of children from the home. Third, the definitions imply that there is a variation in the intensity of service which can be readily observed. The service model in many rural communities may consist of the family-centered case management model while utilizing certain components of the other two models whenever appropriate. During a crisis, for example, the worker may visit the family four times a week during a two-week period; afterwards, the worker may continue to work with the family on a less intensive basis for several months.

When defining a family preservation service, program developers will need to determine which model is closest to the program being designed. If caseload size and service duration are important program components, the program designers and evaluators will need to assess whether these parameters also apply to family-based services provided by tribes or Indian nonprofit providers. Is it appropriate and culturally relevant to provide a short-term intensive service? Are longer models more acceptable to the community? Do the service programs incorporate aspects of different models? What standards should be used by evaluators to measure whether the program model is being implemented as designed?

Given that services are provided in a small community among people who know each other, perhaps length of service will not be defined by case closure. Perhaps, as is more commonly found in the medical profession, a case is either active or inactive—that is a family is receiving services or not receiving services but could receive services at any moment. Furthermore, as discussed above, in a community where a specific worker may be providing all services to a family, it may be difficult to determine when intensive services and when other services are being provided.

DATA COLLECTION

In order to minimize the burden on workers and reduce the costs of evaluation, one evaluation approach uses the case record as the source of data. Information in the case record can serve a dual function of providing the case worker with immediate information on the family and the evaluator with data which can be aggregated to describe the program. Most evaluations would supplement such data collection with interviews with staff and program directors, as well as other relevant persons, in order to get an overall picture of the program and program goals.

This section provides a list of data elements which can be used as a checklist for program developers. Many are standard elements used by evaluators. Each agency can review the list and determine which data elements are useful and which ones are not. Some of the cultural and contextual issues which might arise and need to be reviewed are discussed. The data elements are gathered during the various stages of the service delivery process:

- Referral/Intake
- Assessment
- Service Planning
- Providing Services
- Termination and Follow-up

Figure 1 on page 109, *Summary of Suggested Data Elements,* presents the data elements which are discussed.

FIGURE 1
SUMMARY OF SUGGESTED DATA ELEMENTS

Referral/Intake
  reason for referral
  referral source
  date of referral
  current location of child
  reason child at risk of removal
  degree of imminency of removal
  past history of placements
  additional eligibility factors
  legal status of child
  voluntary or court ordered
    service
  referral decision
  date of decision
  date of first contact
  staff assigned to case

Assessment
  For each household member:
  relationship to primary caretaker
  age
  sex
  marital status
  tribal enrollment
  clan membership (if applicable)

on/off reservation
current location (at home, in
  hospital, etc.)
employment status
education level achieved
other services being received
assessment tool used

Service Planning
  services to be provided
  ancillary services to be provided
    by other providers
  service goals and objectives
  planned time frame of the service

Providing Services
  types of services provided
  frequency (in incidents of service)
  amount of service (in hours)
  service duration (in days)
  number and amount of direct
    contacts
  number and amount of collateral
    contacts
  amount of travel time

Termination and Follow-up
  date of last contact
    date of termination
  progress or lack of progress on
    goals
  critical incidents which occurred
    during service
  recommendations for ongoing
    services
  reason for termination
  client satisfaction with service
    program

Outcomes
  period of follow-up
  case status at time of follow-up
  reason for case closure
  additional reports of abuse/neglect
  results of investigations
  number of placement incidents
  type of placement(s)
  duration of placement(s)
  reason for placement(s)

Referral/Intake

Most programs record the circumstances which lead to a referral and the decision that is made at intake. The program should have clearly written objectives that can be defined in terms of types of clients to be served and/or outcomes for clients. An example of a client-defined objective might be: To serve 40 families whose children have been physically abused and are at risk of removal due to this abuse. An example of an outcome-defined objective might be: To prevent placement of 80 children who have been referred for placement due to abuse and/or neglect. At the referral stage it should be determined whether the referral meets the program eligibility criteria.

Items of particular interest in evaluating family preservation programs are:

- reason for referral
- referral source
- date of referral
- current location of child
- reason child at risk of removal
- degree of imminency of removal
- past history of placements
- additional eligibility factors
- legal status of child
- voluntary or court ordered service
- referral decision
- date of decision
- date of first contact
- staff assigned to case

Implementing a program might raise the following questions with regard to intake/referral and the data elements collected at this point.

- Is there a crisis in the family or has the family been identified as being in need of services but not at crisis?

- Has a culturally appropriate tool been used to determine whether the child is at risk of removal?

- Has the concept of removal from the home been defined in culturally appropriate terms? Should "location of the child" be concerned with whether the child is with biological parents, relatives, non-relatives etc., or whether she/he is in a stable environment regardless of kinship relationships?

- Does the program attempt to reach the family within a short period of time, and, therefore, should the evaluator be interested in the date of first contact, or is this not of concern to the program?

- What factors are involved in case assignment? Has a worker who is a clan member or family member been assigned to the case? Has someone who has worked with the family for a long period of time been assigned, or is there a new worker?

Evaluators may look at such factors as whether there are clear eligibility criteria and whether these criteria are applied at the referral/intake phase of the case. If the program is designed to prevent placement, past histories of placement have been shown to be highly relevant to outcomes (Fraser, Pecora, & Haapala 1988; National Resource Center on Family Based Services 1988).

Assessment

Family Data.
During or soon after intake, most case records include data on the characteristics of the adult and child members of the family, as well as the household itself.

The household composition is usually noted; and, for each person in the family case, the following demographic information is commonly collected:

- relationship to primary caretaker
- age
- sex
- marital status
- tribal enrollment
- clan membership (if applicable)
- on/off reservation
- current location (at home, in hospital, etc.)
- employment status
- education level achieved
- other services being received

If services are being provided to a family with an open case, much of the data may already be available. The evaluator may also need to consider the number of family members to be included in information collection. Changes in family composition should be noted.

Family Strengths and Problems.
In addition to demographic data, service programs use different types of assessment when diagnosing the problems of the family. Areas for assessment may include: parental strengths and weaknesses, parental attitudes, adult disabilities, child behavior, school functioning, interpersonal relationships, and environmental/economic stressors. Several tools are available, but there has been little done in terms of culturally relevant tools for Native American families.

Horejsi (1989 B), in conjunction with several associates, has undertaken to review one risk assessment tool in terms of interpreting behavior to assess risk of abuse or neglect of a child. He has annotated the Montana Child Risk Assessment Instrument which is based upon the Illinois Risk Assessment Matrix. He makes several points which may be useful in considering the cultural relevance of other assessment tools.

- A child receiving little supervision from a biological parent may be cared for and supervised by several other adults. Children are seen as the responsibility of many persons.

- Parents may be very fearful of CPS investigations (or other child welfare workers) since they have heard many stories of unpleasant and even tragic interventions by social workers. Adults may be excessively reticent due to such fear. Even willing and cooperative parents may appear to the worker to be passive.

  When considering the ability of a family to access other services, the political climate of the reservation may need to be considered, since political connections may determine access to services.

He makes the additional point that collecting assessment information may be difficult.

Given the Native American tradition of noninterference, relatives, friends and neighbors may be unwilling to talk about the parent/caretaker under investigation. . . . interfamilial conflicts and long standing family feuds can interfere with the conduct of a thorough and fair investigation (Horesji 1989 B, p. 10).

112

For evaluation purposes, one or more instruments that can be uniformly used for all clients and can measure change is most useful. Some family-oriented programs like to use Goal Attainment Scales. From an evaluation perspective, these are difficult to use because they are idiosyncratic to each family; but in combination with other tools, they can be used successfully.

The features which should be considered when choosing an assessment tool are reviewed, using four tools as examples. The tools discussed are:

- Strengths and Weaknesses Interview Guide
- Child Well-Being Scales
- What are the Signs of Alcoholism?
- Adult-Adolescent Parenting Inventory

The *Strengths and Weaknesses Interview Guide* is included in the model curriculum developed by the Northwest Indian Child Welfare Institute (1984). It is a method of organizing descriptive information on a family. For each of the following areas—family, social, emotional, intellectual, self-help, economic, and physical—the worker writes down the strengths and weaknesses observed and any questions which may arise at that time. One could include other areas or be more specific, depending upon the nature of the service and the needs of the family. The advantage of this approach is that it is relatively easy for caseworkers to use. The disadvantage is that it is difficult to quantify the descriptive data if one wants to compare different families in a caseload. If a tool which is primarily descriptive is chosen, a method of quantifying the information in the tool should be developed.

The *Child Well-Being Scales* were developed by Magura and Moses for the Child Welfare League of America to capture both strengths and weaknesses of a family on many different dimensions, including those mentioned above and others (Magura & Moses 1986). For each item, a scale is provided which can be used to rate the family; each point on the scale is described in detail. An example of the scale on parental consistency of discipline is given below.

1. *High Consistency.* Parent/guardian always follows through on promised rewards and punishments with children; rarely will contradict herself or himself; children know what to expect; punishments fit behavior.

113

2. *Marginal consistency, but open to improvement.* Parent/guardian does not always follow through on sanctions. Sometimes will contradict herself or himself, but makes corrective efforts when inconsistencies are brought to attention. Consistency is understood and valued, but parent/guardian sometimes forgets, acts impulsively, etc.

3. *Marginal consistency, but not open to improvement.* Same as description for (2) above, except that children do not always know what to expect; and parent/guardian seems indifferent to this.

4. *Low consistency.* Parent/guardian often reacts indiscriminately or inconsistently to children's behavior; punishments often do not fit behavior. Parent/guardian may be hostile when problems are brought to attention.

In using these scales in a tribal setting, each item should be reviewed and those which are most relevant chosen for use. Additional scales might also be developed. The advantages of these scales are that they have been widely used and that the descriptors help workers to rate a family. Furthermore, measurable comparisons between families are facilitated. The disadvantages are that it has not been used widely with Indian families and that there are some areas, including alcoholism, which are not well covered. (Figure 2 on page 115, *List of Items from the Child Well-Being Scales,* cites all the items.)

The checklist, *What are the Signs of Alcoholism,* was developed by the National Council on Alcoholism and is included in the curriculum developed by the Northwest Indian Child Welfare Institute (1984). "Yes" answers may indicate alcoholism. The 26 questions refer to different stages of alcoholism. Some of the questions are:

- Do you occasionally drink heavily after a disappointment, a quarrel, or when the boss gives you a hard time?

- When you have trouble or feel under pressure, do you always drink more heavily than usual?

- Are you secretly irritated when your family or friends discuss your drinking?

- Do you try to avoid family or close friends while you are drinking?

114

FIGURE 2
LIST OF ITEMS FROM THE CHILD WELL-BEING SCALES

For parents:

Physical Health Care
Nutrition and Diet
Clothing
Personal Hygiene
Household Furnishings
Overcrowding
Household Sanitation
Security of Residence
Availability of Utilities
Physical Safety in Home
Mental Health Care
Supervision of Young Child (under 13)
Supervision of Teenage Children
Arrangements for Substitute Care
Money Management
Parental Capacity for Child Care
Parental Relations
Continuity of Parenting
Parental Recognition of Problems
Parental Motivation To Solve Problems
Parental Cooperation with Case Planning Problems
Support for Principal Caretaker

Availability/Accessibility of Services
Acceptance of Affection for Children
Approval of Children
Expectations of Children
Consistency of Discipline
Teaching/Stimulating Children

For each child:

Physical Discipline
Deliberate Deprivation of Food/Water
Physical Confinement or Restriction
Deliberate Locking Out
Sexual Abuse
Threat of Abuse
Economic Exploitation
Protection from Abuse
Adequacy of Education
Academic Performance
School Attendance
Children's Family Relations
Children's Misconduct
Coping Behavior of Children

115

- Do more people seem to be treating you unfairly without good reason?

- Do you sometimes feel very depressed and wonder whether life is worth living?

- Do you get terribly frightened after you have been drinking heavily?

This assessment tool, while specialized, has particular utilization for workers who are planning in-home services. "Yes" answers may indicate that further assessment and treatment may be necessary for the family prior to providing in-home services. This assessment tool is an example of a highly focused tool that, however, can be used to compare cases as well as shed additional light on the necessary casework which needs to be conducted. Responses could be compared on specific items and in terms of overall scores. A disadvantage is that cultural responses to alcoholism are not well incorporated into the instrument, and substance abuse issues are not considered.

The *Adult-Adolescent Parenting Inventory* was developed by Bavolek (1984) to assess high-risk parenting and child-rearing attitudes among adult and adolescent populations. Four main areas are assessed through this instrument: developmental expectations of children, belief in the use of corporal punishment, empathetic awareness of children's needs, and reversing parent-child family roles. For each of the 32 items, the respondent circles the extent to which they agree or disagree with the statement. Some of the items are:

- Parents spoil their children by picking them up and comforting them when they cry.

- Children should not be expected to talk before the age of one year.

- Young children should be aware of ways to comfort their parents after a hard day's work.

- Parents who encourage communication with their children only end up listening to complaints.

- Children should never be forced to respect parental authority.

The instrument has been used with several thousand individuals, and a method of scoring has been developed. However, the cultural relevance of this questionnaire has not been tested. Tribal and nonprofit service providers will need to consider whether the items and scoring are relevant to the American Indian community.

Assessment tools are important for many different reasons. With regard to evaluation, they become important as a common means of describing different families, independent of a specific worker. The objective is to convey a certain amount of information that different workers or evaluators can use. In selecting an assessment tool for use in both service planning and in evaluation, the following questions should be addressed:

- Does the tool capture data which is thought to be important by the community?

- Does the tool address culturally relevant socialization values?

- Can the tool be used by different staff members and can training be designed for workers? Will workers need special skills in order to conduct the assessment?

- Do certain areas of the assessment discuss sensitive issues which will dissuade a family from participating instead of encourage a family to receive services? Can these areas be eliminated or modified?

- Can the program maintain the confidentiality of information?

- Has the tool been used in other sites, and is it considered a reliable measure of strengths and weaknesses?

- Does the tool provide information which can be quantified for aggregated analysis?

Evaluators often use assessment tools to compare families in terms of types of problems or level of problem. The use of a standardized tool enables the program implementer and evaluator to decide whether certain families do better in the program than other families. Such information can lead to program enhancement.

Service Planning

A service plan is dependent upon several different factors:

- problem(s) of the family
- strengths of the family
- skills of the worker
- resources available to the worker
- requirements of other agencies involved

In family preservation programs, items of interest to evaluators include:

- services to be provided,
- ancillary services to be provided by other providers,
- service goals and objectives, and
- planned time frame of the service.

In order to plan and record the delivery of different services, a typology of services needs to be developed. Figure 3 on page 119, *Typology of Services - A*, gives one typology of service which can be reviewed. Figure 4 on page 120, *Typology of Services - B*, provides a shorter typology of services based on the reporting requirements for the Social Services Block Grant Program to states.

Deciding on the goals of the intervention may be more difficult. The program designer will need to discuss the theory of the service and what practice-based goals will be used. Clearly, such goals must be culturally based. Some workers may find that more traditional families will not accept goal-oriented interventions very easily and that the goals must evolve in an unstated way rather than be presented at the point of service planning. Measuring the achievement of service goals may require qualitative techniques rather than quantitative techniques on the part of the evaluator.

Providing Services

Evaluators are concerned with the nature of the services which are provided. Indian agencies which provide mental health services are familiar with keeping detailed records on their interactions with clients. Agencies which only provide child and family services may be less used to providing this amount of data and may be more accustomed to entering remarks into a service journal.

FIGURE 3
TYPOLOGY OF SERVICES - A

100.	ASSESSMENT	402.	Child Therapy
101.	Assessment of Family/Child	403.	Individual Counseling
102.	Psychological Testing	404.	Family Counseling/Therapy
103.	Psychiatric Evaluation	405.	Group Counseling
104.	Child Protection Team	406.	Peer Support Group
		407.	Marital Counseling
200.	CASE PLANNING AND	408.	Family Planning
	SUPERVISION	409.	Drug Abuse Counseling
201.	Case Consultation and	410.	Alcohol Abuse Counseling
	Supervision	411.	Detoxification Services
202.	Psychiatric Case Consultation	412.	Financial Management/
203.	Case Record Keeping		Budgeting
204.	Case Planning with Client	413.	Parental Skills Training
		414.	Vocational/Employment
300.	COORDINATION WITH		Counseling
	COLLATERALS	415.	Tutoring/Educational Skills
301.	Coordination with Referring		Development
	Agency	416.	School Attendance/Behavior
302.	Court Preparation and/or	417.	Follow-up Counseling
	Appearance		
303.	Arranging for Other Services	500.	PLACEMENT SERVICES
304.	Advocacy	501.	Emergency Shelter
		502.	Relative Home
400.	COUNSELING/THERAPY	503.	Foster Family Home
401.	Crisis Intervention/Support	504.	Group Home

505.	Residential Treatment Center		
506.	Mental Health Facility		
507.	Juvenile Detention		
508.	Pre-adoptive Home		
600.	SUPPORT SERVICES		
601.	Parent Aide		
602.	Homemaker		
603.	Chore Services		
604.	Day Care		
605.	Respite Care		
606.	Recreation		
607.	Visiting Nurse		
700.	CONCRETE SERVICES		
701.	Transportation		
702.	Food		
703.	Clothing		
704.	Furniture/Supplies		
705.	Financial Assistance		
706.	Moving Assistance		
707.	Medical/Dental Care		
800.	OTHER		

119

FIGURE 4
TYPOLOGY OF SERVICES - B
(Adapted from the Social Service Block Grant Program:
New Reporting Requirements)
Source: Federal Register, Vol. 55, No. 66, April 5, 1990

Case Management Services
Counseling Services
Day Care Services
Employment, Education and Training Services
Family Planning Services
Foster Care Services
Health Related Services
Home Based Services
Home Delivered Meals
Housing Services
Information and Referral Services
Legal Services
Pregnancy and Parenting Services to
 Young Parents
Prevention and Intervention Services
Protective Services for Children
Recreational Services
Residential Treatment Services
Special Services for the Developmentally Disabled,
  the Blind, and the Physically Disabled
Special Services for Juvenile Delinquents
Substance Abuse Services
Transportation
Other Services

If it is decided that detailed service data will be collected in a systematic fashion that can be easily analyzed by evaluators, there are two basic approaches to collecting information on the services provided.

Approach A. Workers check off a list of services which they provide. No attempt is made to account for the amount of time they spend on the different types of services.

Approach B. Workers keep detailed daily logs of the services which they provide. At a minimum, they record each time a service is provided and the amount of time spent in providing that service. Additionally, they may record which members of the family were present when services were provided, the location of service, the staff who provided the service, and the amount of travel time spent in delivering that service.

Some agencies may choose a compromise type of recording which calls for the worker to put a check mark next to the type of service every time the service is provided. For example, one could learn that Elaine Smith provided transportation to a family seven times (frequency of service incidents), which is more than knowing that Elaine provided transportation services to the family and less than knowing that she provided 30 hours of service (amount of service provided), over a period of 50 days (duration of service).

Agencies will need to decide what level of data they will collect on the services provided. If it is determined that detailed recording is too much of a burden on all cases, workers could collect data on a sample of cases, i.e., a worker might keep detailed records on every fifth case. Thus a program could still describe the nature of the service in terms of number of contacts, or number of hours of direct service and number of hours of collateral service. Such data are also useful for program designers as they determine what are the resources needed to deliver a service.

Termination and Follow-Up

At termination, the worker has the opportunity to record any changes that have occurred with the family. The assessment instrument used at intake may be used also at termination in order to measure change in the condition, behavior, or attitudes of the family. Additional information of interest to the evaluator include:

- date of last contact,
- date of termination,
- progress or lack of progress on goals,
- critical incidents which occurred during service,
- recommendations for ongoing services,
- reason for termination, and
- client satisfaction with service program.

As discussed above, the program will decide whether the services are to be time limited or not. If services are not time limited, the program may want to review the progress of the family at six-month intervals, and the evaluation could consider the amount of progress at specified review periods.

In order to assess the impact of family preservation services, evaluators and program designers are interested in outcomes which occur for a period after termination. Since most family preservation services have the goal of keeping children at home, one outcome might be whether the child remains at home for a period of time. Periods of at least six months after termination are usually considered. Items of interest include:

- period of follow-up,
- case status at time of follow-up,
- reason for case closure,
- additional reports of abuse/neglect,
- results of investigations,
- number of placement incidents,
- type of placement(s),
- duration of placement(s), and
- reason for placement(s).

A program might also want to consider other indices of family well-being, such as school behavior, runaway behavior, involvement with juvenile court, etc. The scope of the information gathered at follow-up is largely dependent upon the resources of the program. Programs need to consider whether follow-up information is readily available and whether there are staff resources to examine the data.

TYPES OF ANALYSES

Once the information is collected in the case record, the program director and/or evaluator can review the data to provide descriptive statistics.

Some of the questions which are most commonly asked are:

- How many families and children were served?
- What were the characteristics of the families and children served?
- What were the referral reasons and referral sources?
- What were the goals of service?
- Were these goals achieved?
- What types of services were provided to families?
- How much service was provided to families?
- What were the outcomes of service?
- Based on the outcomes of service, has the program design or operations been revised?

CONCLUSION

The design and incorporation of suitable evaluation procedures is extremely important. Paying attention to key cultural factors and employing relevant evaluation practices, such as relying on the case record, will allow the Indian Child Welfare field to conduct evaluations and advance the development and implementation of family preservation services.

REFERENCES

Bavolek, S. J. (1985). *Adult-adolescent parenting inventory.* Illinois: Family Development Associates.

Child Welfare League of America. (1990). *Standards for services to strengthen and preserve families with children.* Washington, D. C.

Fraser, M., Pecora, P., & Haapala, D. (Eds.) (1988). *Families in crisis: Findings from the family-based intensive treatment project.* Utah: University of Utah, Graduate School of Social Work.

Horejsi, C. (1989 A). *Traditional Native American cultures and contemporary U.S. society: A comparison.* Unpublished manuscript. Montana: Department of Social Work, University of Montana.

Horejsi, C. (1989 B). *Risk assessment and the Native American family.* Unpublished manuscript. Montana: Department of Social Work, University of Montana.

Magura, S., & Moses, B. S. (1986). *Outcome measures for child welfare services.* Washington, D. C.: Child Welfare League of America.

Merryfield, M. M. (1985). The challenge of cross-cultural evaluation: Some views from the field. In M. Q. Patton (Ed.), *Culture and evaluation: New directions for program evaluation.* California: Jossey-Bass Inc.

National Resource Center on Family Based Services. (1988). *An analysis of factors contributing to failure in family-based child welfare services in eleven family-based agencies: Final report.* Iowa.

Northwest Indian Child Welfare Institute. (1984). *Trainers' guide for module II: Protective services for Indian children.* Oregon: Parry Center for Children.

Office of Human Development Services. (1990). Fiscal year 1990 coordinated discretionary funds program. *Federal Register.* Vol. 55, No. 46, Mar. 8, 1990. Washington, D. C.: U. S. Government Printing Office.

Patton, M. Q. (1985). Cross-cultural generalizations. In M. Q. Patton (Ed.), *Culture and evaluation. New directions for program evaluation.* California: Jossey-Bass Inc.

Plantz, M. C., Hubbell, R., & Dobrec, A. (1988). *Indian child welfare: A status report*—Final report of the survey of Indian Child Welfare and implementation of the Indian Child Welfare Act and Section 428 of the Adoption Assistance and Child Welfare Act of 1980. Washington, D. C.: CSR, Inc.

Yuan, Y. T., & Rivest, M. (1990). *Preserving families: Evaluation resources for practitioners and policymakers.* New Jersey: Sage Publications.

ABOUT THE CONTRIBUTORS

Marc Mannes is Senior Program Manager at the American Indian Law Center, Inc., Albuquerque, New Mexico. He will be joining the Department of Social Work faculty, New Mexico State University, Las Cruces, New Mexico, as an assistant professor beginning in the fall of 1990.

Nadine W. Tafoya is currently in private practice in Northern New Mexico where she specializes in community mental health and Indian Child Welfare issues.

John P. Ronnau is an assistant professor, Department of Social Work, New Mexico State University, Las Cruces, New Mexico.

June C. Lloyd is a family-centered services specialist, Arkansas Division of Child & Family Services, Little Rock, Arkansas.

Alvin L. Sallee is professor and academic department head, Department of Social Work, New Mexico State University, Las Cruces, New Mexico.

Patricia J. Shannon is a college assistant professor, Department of Social Work, New Mexico State University, Las Cruces, New Mexico.

Ying-Ying T. Yuan is Vice-President of Walter R. McDonald & Associates, Inc. She has evaluated family preservation service programs in California and Connecticut.